D1743036

Good and Evil

An individual interpretation of *The Secret Doctrine*
by Helena P. Blavatsky

Tatyana N. Mickushina

Good and Evil

An individual interpretation of *The Secret Doctrine* by Helena P. Blavatsky

Tatyana N. Mickushina

Translated from Russian by
Svetlana Nekrasova

In this book the author illuminates the knowledge given by the Masters through Helena P. Blavatsky in the 19th century and makes an attempt to restore the Truth about the fall of Lucifer, the fall of angels and the fall of humanity.

Websites:
http://sirius-eng.net (English version)
http://sirius-ru.net (Russian version)

ISBN: 1-4536-2684-0
ISBN-13: 9781453626849

Table of Contents

Preface

In the late 90s of the century that belongs to the past now I came across the Teaching of the Ascended Masters. This Teaching was given through a non-commercial American organisation, The Summit Lighthouse and its messengers Mark and Elizabeth Prophet. I read basically all the literature published in Russian on the side of The Summit Lighthouse. I was elated.

I bethought myself that if I could give the world the knowledge I had found in that Teaching, the understanding of Good and Evil, the world would change. It is impossible for it not to change. People simply do not know anything. It is necessary to tell them.

I even started to write a book where I was retelling in my own language the knowledge I had obtained. Two chapters from that book are presented below.

Lucifer's rebellion

The fundamental realignment of the planet took place in the times of the ancient Lemuria. Lucifer, the son of Dawn, who had a high position in the divine hierarchy, allowed himself a rebellion against God. He was a mighty angel, an outstanding personality with a great power of persuasion. He cast doubt upon the Cosmic Law, the Hierarchy of Light, and raised a rebellion against the Universal Plan.

The essence of this rebellion was that he chose service to his ego, his self, rather than to God. Due to his charisma and the logic of persuasion he attracted many followers, "a third of the stars" (Rev.12:4) and made them worship and serve him. This is how this rebellion is described in the *Apocalypse*:

And there was war in heaven. Michael and his angels fought against the dragon, and the dragon and his angels fought back. But he was not strong enough, and they lost their place in heaven. The great dragon was hurled down – that ancient serpent called the devil, or Satan, who leads the whole world astray. He was hurled to the earth, and his angels with him. (Rev. 12:7-9)

The angels of Archangel Michael and Archangel Gabriel managed to free the highest spheres from the rebels. Lucifer and his angels lost their Light and found a shelter for themselves on planet Earth. Since then Lucifer has been named devil, his helper and his right hand – Satan, and his angels who followed him – fallen angels.

The source of energy and the Light in the Universe is God. Those who renounce God are deprived of energy. But energy is needed in order to exist. What would they do? Light can be taken away from those who possess it. For the fallen angels to find energy is a matter of life and death.

If a person is in harmony with God, he receives Divine energy for implementing the goals of God. In the twilight of history the Earth was inhabited by mankind that settled in general on the continent Lemuria situated in the place which is covered now by the Indian and the Pacific Oceans. Humanity possessed the mysteries of Cosmos which were later on either lost or possessed by only a narrow circle of the initiated.

At the helm of the state there was a tsar who was in the supreme holy orders at the same time. The Lemurians venerated their sovereign and believed he was a deity, but they worshipped the One, who was invisible.

On the continents and in the colonies situated in America, India and China God was worshipped as Father-Mother. The beliefs of ancient India have partly retained the holy cult of the Mother which was widespread in Lemuria and then gradually forgotten in the course of the fall of mankind. There was no contradiction between science and religion, science being a practical appendix to the religious truths and occupying itself with the description of these truths with the help of symbols and glyphs.

When the fallen angels were thrown to the Earth, the innocent humanity, unaware of self-will, then faced statements that were strange to humans: why worship somebody whom we neither see nor hear? Only that which surrounds us is real, so isn't it better to concentrate on getting pleasures from life?

The fall of humanity

T hus, in accordance with the cosmic law, after having arrived on the Earth the fallen angels had to be embodied in human bodies. The bodies that we see represent only a cover, skin clothes for the soul. In order to exist one needs energy. If there is no chance to obtain energy directly from God one has to contrive and take it from the surrounding people. For this purpose one needs to bring people to a state of disharmony and put them into confusion. This can be achieved with the help of engendering within them such thoughts and feelings that were disharmonious with God.

Why should we worship somebody whom we neither see nor hear? Why not use our life for getting pleasures for ourselves?

People began to abstract themselves from the Divine Truths and to act in the way they were taught by their crafty whisperers. Doing so, they were losing their Light, and on the horizontal level it was picked up by the fallen.

Further, the law of retribution or the law of human karma automatically came into force. If we allow non-divine thoughts and feelings in our consciousness, if we perform ungodly actions, we inevitably encounter situations in our lives when we have to make a choice and to demonstrate that very quality which distorted. For example, let's say we allowed a doubt in the existence of God within our mind. We will have to display our faith in much worse conditions.

As we already know from the description of the Golden Age, people had an ability to walk upon the water. When they lost their faith, this quality was lost, as well as the ability to materialise food and objects.

5

These abilities were gradually withdrawn and so it was necessary to believe in God again, in the justice of His Law, but to do so became much more difficult.

The consciousness of people was growing narrower little by little and became mortal. There appeared a veil separating the higher Divine octaves from the world of shapes. The connection between the immortal Divine part of man and his lower consciousness was lost, and this consciousness was gradually limited only by the world that was perceptible to the human eye.

And a lie of the fallen was continually penetrating people's ears – that people were their own gods and that they would force nature and God Himself to bow to them, and that in this struggle the battle would be won by the strong and the choice of the end covered the choice of the means.

And gradually the feeling of love towards all creation ranging from God to the surrounding people and even bugs was substituted by extreme enmity, jealousy, spite and lust.

The fall was rapid. In a few centuries time there was no man on the planet who would follow the former code of behaviour.

Necessary explanations

I t would seem to have been written correctly. But something stopped me from doing further work on the book. It is not easy to explain. It is at the level of intuition. It seemed to me that there was a hidden agenda behind all this or maybe something was little-understood by me.

At any rate I broke off my work.

It was the year 2002. It should be said that from 2002 I have been practising meditation. So, in the course of meditations I began to obtain understanding and knowledge that differed from the knowledge written in the Teaching of the Ascended Masters. That was another point of view on the fallen angels and Lucifer.

I thought I had followed the wrong path. During the meditations my consciousness perceived new information, and after the meditations I regularly wrote down everything that was happening, but my external consciousness refused to accept the new information.

I was left in peace, but only for short while. One year hence the information started coming again.

Then I began to seek other, external sources of information that could authenticate the knowledge I received in the subtle plane.

Many years ago I read *The Secret Doctrine* by H.P. Blavatsky. And I felt a need to go to this book again.

Those who have ever read this book can imagine how hard it is to understand the sense of what is written in it. The narration is deliberately entangled and obscured in order to disorient the profane.

I set about reading it a few times. I understood that *The Secret Doctrine* was in harmony with the knowledge I received in the subtle plane, but the sense of the written escaped me. And it was only in the year 2004 when I was in the Altai that I suddenly felt that I started to understand, maybe not everything, but at least to a certain extent.

At the same time I felt a need to represent in my own words what I had managed to realise. For some reason it is important to do this now.

A glimpse of H.P. Blavatsky

It may be said that Blavatsky wrote her works to the dictation of Master El Morya[1] and Master Kuthumi[2]. It may also be said that these works were written with the help of the gifts of the Holy Spirit. That was an attempt of the Mahatmas from the East to give a part of the secret knowledge that had been passed down by the initiated from generation to generation during many millions of years.

Here is how El Morya and Kuthumi themselves present, through Blavatsky, the essence of the conducted work:

"The reader can never be too often reminded that, as the abundant quotations from various old Scriptures prove, these teachings are as old as the world; and that the present work is a simple attempt to render, in modern language and in a phraseology with which the scientific and educated student is familiar, archaic Genesis and History as taught in certain Asiatic centres of esoteric learning. They must be accepted or rejected on their own merits, fully or partially; but not before they have been carefully compared with the corresponding theological dogmas and the modern scientific theories and speculations.

---

[1] El Morya Khan, a Rajput prince. In 1875 he worked on the foundation of the Theosophical Society together with Kuthumi, Djwal Kul, Serapis Bey, Saint Germain and others.

[2] Kuthumi. He is also known as K.H., Koot Hoomi Lal Singh, nineteenth-century Kashmiri Brahman (Brahmin), Shigatse, Tibet.

One feels a serious doubt whether, with all its intellectual acuteness, our age is destined to discover in each western nation even one solitary uninitiated scholar or philosopher capable of fully comprehending the spirit of archaic philosophy."[3]

Elena F. Pisareva[4] explains why Blavatsky was chosen:

"She was a genuine messenger from the East who came to illuminate the consciousness of people of the world. In the 14th century a great wise man, an enlightener and a reformer of Buddhism, Tsongkhapa, reminded the wise men of Tibet and the Himalayas of the provision of a very ancient law. This law established the need of commensuration of the opposite yet equally true principles – THE TRUTH MUST BE KEPT SECRET, THE TRUTH MUST BE DIVULGED – since for an unenlightened person untimely knowledge is as fatal as light for one who was staying in darkness. Tsongkhapa reminded them that at the end of each century an attempt must be made to enlighten the people of the West who cared exclusively about power and material welfare. And then an attempt was made to spread the light and to send a messenger.

"This matter was considered in the Buddhist monastery Shoh near Shigatse situated on the border of China and Tibet. There was a question as to with whom it was possible to send a message to the incredulous and

---

[3] From here onwards the quotations from *The Secret Doctrine* (marked in **bold italics**) are taken from the edition: The Secret Doctrine by H.P. Blavatsky – Vol. 2 – THEOSOPHICAL UNIVERSITY PRESS ASCII EDITION (SCANNED AND EDITED FROM THE ORIGINAL EDITION OF 1888) – P. 449.

[4] The passage is cited from the preface to the Russian edition of the book *The Mahatma Letters*. – Samara, 1993.

haughty people of the West. It was almost unanimously resolved to give up such an attempt, since the West had lost the ability to perceive and to understand the true ancient Teaching.

Morya

Kuthumi

"However, two people agreed to follow the instructions of Tsongkhapa. They were Morya, a descendant of the rulers of Punjab, and Kuthumi from Kashmir. They undertook the responsibility to choose a messenger and to send him to the West in order to spread there the philosophy of the East and to reveal some of secrets relating to the nature of man.

"Their choice fell on H.P. Blavatsky who was karmically linked with Teacher Morya.

"She was chosen due to her gift as a medium, due to her supernatural abilities which she had manifested since her childhood. These abilities enabled Mahatmas Morya and Kuthumi to mentally communicate with her over a distance. She was chosen also for her unselfish faith, unfathomable love for knowledge, for that fire that prompts some beings to raise the spirited torch of their reason higher and higher, even with the risk of dying amidst the darkness that surrounds us."

I will cite some more passages confirming the fact that Blavatsky did not write her works by herself, she was just an amenable tool that the Masters used. Here is a passage from the memoirs of Vera Jelihovsky, a full sister of Blavatsky, which dates back to the moment of the beginning of Blavatsky's work on "Isis Unveiled" during her stay in America:

"Allusions have started to appear more and more often and pronouncedly in her letters that what she is writing does not belong to her; that she herself does not understand the things happening to her. But it is quite evident to her that she speaks and writes about scientific and abstract objects not from herself – because she 'has no clue' about them, – but that 'someone who knows everything dictates' to her and indoctrinates her.

"These strange manifestations of scientific knowledge that flashed upon her out of nowhere at the age of forty, in conjunction with such extraordinary indications on some kind of 'possession', seriously troubled Blavatsky's family… For some time they were even apprehensive about her mind.

" 'Tell me, my dear', – she wrote to her aunt[5], – 'are you interested in physiological-psychological secrets? But all this is just an amazing puzzle for any physiologist. There are very learned members in our society (e.g. professor Wilder, an archeologist-orientalist), and all of them roll up to me with questions and stick to the opinion that I know better than they – both eastern languages and sciences, positive and

---

[5] To Nadezhda Andreevna Fadeeva, her mother's sister.

abstract. But this is a fact, and there is no arguing with a fact just like there is no arguing with a large fist!.. So, do tell me how could it happen that I, after having been completely untaught until the years of maturity, as you know, all of a sudden became a phenomenon of wisdom in the eyes of the people who are real learned scholars?.. But this is an impenetrable mystery!.. I am a psychological puzzle, a rebus and an enigma for the future generations, a sphinx... Just think that I, who did not learn absolutely anything in life, I, who had no idea about chemistry, physics or zoology, – am writing now dissertations about all these things. I dispute with the scientists and come off with honour... I am not joking, I'm serious. I am scared because I don't understand how all this is done!.. Everything I read seems familiar to me now... I find errors in the articles of the scientists, in the lectures of Tindal, Herbert Spenser, Huxley and others...From morning till night professors, doctors, and theologians spend time at my place. They launch into arguments – and I happen to be right. But where is this all from? Have I been substituted, I wonder?'

"At the same time she sent clippings from various newspapers which confirmed her verbal and printed victories over a range of authorities and, besides, announced to the world a mass of such unbelievable facts about the mystic phenomenal capabilities and talents of the founder of the Theosophical Society that it was impossible for reasonable people to believe in them."[6]

---

[6] V.P. Jelihovsky – *Radda-bai, or the truth about Blavatsky*. The entire article is available in Russian at the following location: http://www.theosophy.ru/lib/raddabai.htm

And one more passage, unveiling the mystery about how *The Secret Doctrine* was written:

"I am very busy on 'Secret D.' The thing in New York (she meant the pictures of psychographic clairvoyance – 'suggestions' – as she called them) is repeated – only far clearer and better. I begin to think it shall vindicate us. Such pictures, panoramas, scenes, antediluvian dramas, with all that! Never saw or heard better."[7]

And the last passage to illustrate the purpose of the attempt I am undertaking in order to restore the Truth. A well-known historical fact is that, while staying in London, at the end of her life, Blavatsky published a magazine called *Lucifer* which in its turn brought a storm about her ears and laid her open to accusations. H.P. Blavatsky wrote the following as an excuse:

"Why did you flash out at me for my having titled my magazine *Lucifer*?.. This is a beautiful title! Lux, Lucis – light; ferre – to bring: 'Lightbearer' – what can be superior?.. It is only owing to Milton's *Paradise Lost* [8] that Lucifer became a synonym of a fallen spirit. The first fair deed of my magazine will be to discard the slander of misconception off this name by which ancient Christians called Christ. Hence the Greek Eosphoros, or the Latin Lucifer, as this is the name of the morning star, a nunciate of the bright sunshine. Didn't Christ say about himself: 'I, Jesus… am the

---

[7] V.P. Jelihovsky – *Radda-bai, or the truth about Blavatsky*. The entire article is available in Russian at the following location: http://www.theosophy.ru/lib/raddabai.htm

[8] John Milton (1608-1674) – an English poet and civil servant. During the English Bourgeois Revolution of the 17th century he was a supporter of the Independents. In the poems *Paradise Lost* (1667) and *Paradise Regained* (1671) he allegorically expressed revolutionary ideas through the Bible's images, raised the question about the right of man to trespass the moral blessed by God.

root… and the bright and Morning Star'. (Rev. St. John 22.16)?.. So may our magazine, like a pale pure star of the dawn, be the precursor of the bright dawn of the truth – a mergence of all the written interpretations into a single and congenial light of the truth!"[9]

The Truth must be divulged.

---

[9] V.P. Jelihovsky – *Radda-bai, or the truth about Blavatsky*. The entire article is available in Russian at the following location: http://www.theosophy.ru/lib/raddabai.htm

The circle of subjects
outlined for review

"There is no Religion higher than Truth" – this phrase is the subtitle of *The Secret Doctrine*, and I will try to follow the Truth no matter how implausible it may seem. So, I intend to review the subject of the appearance of Good and Evil on Earth and the subject of the fallen angels and Lucifer, which is inevitably connected with it.

Any other subjects will be mentioned only in passing and no more than within the limits necessary for the highlighting of the main theme.

My narration will be very schematic, but still I hope that the Truth will be none the worse for that. In any case, the desirous can always go to the fountainhead.

Any reading and any paraphrasing can only be performed through a prism of personal perception, because in order to have your own dry light I still direct you to the fountainhead.

Conformity between the principles of man and Earth

In everything – both in the macrocosm and in the microcosm – the Law of Similarity operates. From the Teaching of the Ascended Masters it is known that man is a complex structure. Apart from the physical body he has three more subtle bodies which surround his body like a nested doll: the astral body, the mental body and the etheric body. Apart from these four lower bodies man has three higher bodies: the Christ Self, the Causal Body and the I AM Presence. The structure of these bodies can be visualised in the form of a Scheme of the I AM Presence as shown in the picture.

The Secret Doctrine uses other names for these bodies, but we will not delve into the specifics of discrepancies now. For our purpose it is enough to realise that man is a complex structure comprised of seven bodies or principles. In conformity with the Law of Similarity our planet must also consist of seven bodies or principles. The conformity between the human's and the planet's principles is shown in the diagram.

The smallest figure in the centre of the chart is the I AM Presence, a particle of God within us. A larger figure represents the four lower bodies: the physical, the emotional, the mental and the etheric ones. The largest figure is the Holy Christ Self (Higher Self). It is holding your hands in its hands. The spheres surrounding the figures represent your causal body.

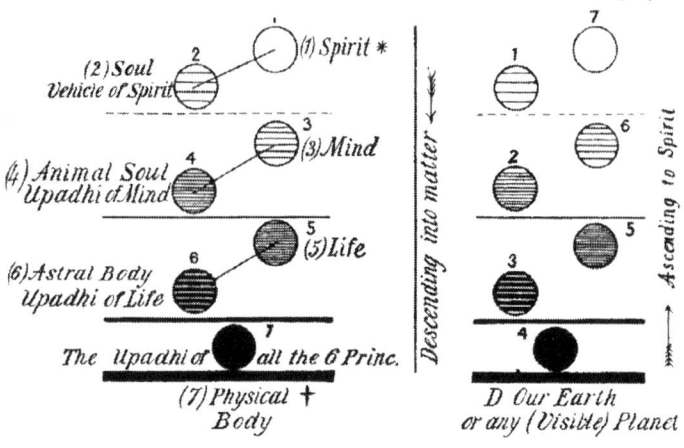

When we speak about a planet, a nascency of a planet in the physical plane takes place in the following way: around a focus in space a gaseous eddy starts to form, then it gradually condenses and becomes solid. But just as how we cannot see the subtle bodies of man with our physical eyes, we cannot see the subtle bodies of Earth or any other planet.

However, everything originates in the more subtle invisible planes and only then everything is manifested in the physical plane.

According to *The Secret Doctrine* life exists on all the seven bodies or globes of Earth or any other planet... Moreover, the monads or Divine foci around which the creation of life takes place (they can be symbolically compared to I AM Presence, an immortal particle in us), were originally brought to our planet from the Moon. The Moon is our ancestress.

The diagram demonstrates in what manner life was brought from the Moon to the Earth. When the lunar globe **A** was concluding its existence, the vital impulse from it was transferred to the globe **A** of the Earth. The same happened with the globes **B, C, D**...

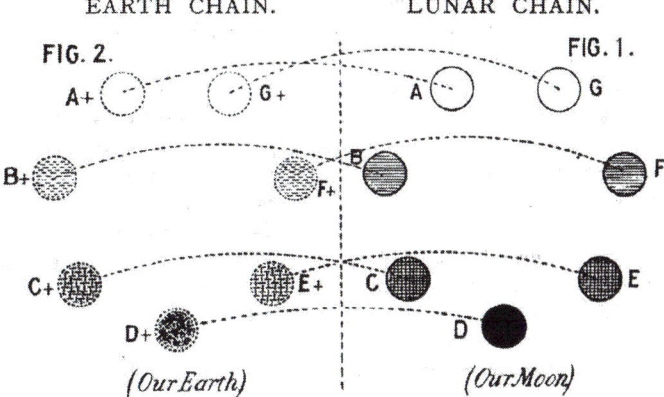

EARTH CHAIN.   LUNAR CHAIN.

FIG. 2.   FIG. 1.

(Our Earth)   *(Our Moon)*

Each monad transferred from the Moon had to pass through its evolution anew, first as a mineral, then as a plant, an animal and, finally, as a human.

Besides, nature adjusted the cycles in such a way that when the vital impulse of the highest class of monads achieved globe **A**, the vital impulse of the mineral life moved to globe **B**. In this manner life waves gradually passed from one globe to another.

Life that exists on the globes belonging to the subtle planes cannot be correspondingly associated with our physical plane. But for our purpose it is important to realise that life exists in many planes and reaches its maximum density on globe **D** – our physical globe.

Apart from the notion of the globes, *The Secret Doctrine* also gives a notion of the rounds. In the course of its development each globe passes through seven rounds. Between all the rounds there exists a period of a partial pralaya, peace, or obscuration when life becomes stock-still and then regenerates anew in the next round.

At present we are on globe **D** in the fourth round – at the lowest point of materiality.

That is all, basically, which we have to know more or less for the further narration, since in the further discourse we will only touch upon our physical globe.

Those who became interested in all these rounds, globes and planet chains can become familiarised with their description in detail in the first volume of *The Secret Doctrine*, in *Esoteric Buddhism* by Sinnett and in *The Mahatma Letters*. I will only say that the narration is deliberately obscured and a part of the information is held back. However, those who get hold of the keys from the subtle plane will manage to understand and reason out the rest of it.

Which period of time the speech is about

et's see now which period of time the speech could be about. During however many years the globes of the Earth were inhabited by the Divine monads.

"On the other hand, it is well to know that no secret was so well preserved and so sacred with the ancients, as that of their cycles and computations. From the Egyptians down to the Jews it was held as the highest sin to divulge anything pertaining to the correct measure of time."[10]

However, in *The Secret Doctrine* the precise figures are given, and I am disposed to believe them. Here they are:

I. From the beginning of cosmic evolution[11], up to the Hindu year Tarana (or 1887)	1,955,884,687 years
II. The (astral) mineral, vegetable and animal kingdoms up to Man, have taken to evolve	300,000,000 years
III. Time, from the first appearance of "Humanity" (on planetary chain)	1,664,500,987 years
IV. The number that elapsed since the "Vaivasvata Manvantara" – or *the human period* – up to the year 1887, is just	18,618,728 years
V. The full period of one Manvantara is	308,448,000 years

---

[10] H.P. Blavatsky, The Secret Doctrine – Vol. 2, Page 396.

[11] The esoteric doctrine says that this "cosmic evolution" refers only to our solar system; while exoteric Hinduism makes the figures refer, if we do not mistake, to the whole Universal System. (The footnote is copied from the book *The Secret Doctrine*)

VI. 14 "Manvantaras" *plus* the period of one Satya Yuga make ONE DAY OF BRAHMA, or **complete Manvantara** and make	4,320,000,000 years 1/3 → 1.444.000.000
Therefore a Maha-Yuga consists of	4,320,000 years[12]
The number of years that passed between the beginning of Kali-Yuga and the year 1887 is	1/3 → 1.444.000 4,989 years

Here are some more figures for better clarity: NUmeloun

	Mortal years:	
360 days of mortals make a year	1	
Krita Yuga contains	1,728,000	= 9
Treta Yuga contains	1,296,000	= 9
Dwapara Yuga contains	864,000	= 9
Kali Yuga contains	432,000	= 9
The total of the said four Yugas constitute a Maha Yuga	4,320,000	= 9
Seventy-one of such Maha-Yugas form the period of the reign of one Manu	306,720,000	= 9
The reign of 14 Manus embraces the duration of 994 Maha-Yugas, which is equal to	4,294,080,000	= 9
Add Sandhis, i.e., intervals between the reign of each Manu, which amount to six Maha-Yugas, equal to	25,920,000	= 9
The total of these reigns and interregnums of 14 Manus, is 1,000 Maha-Yugas, which constitute a Kalpa, i.e., one day of Brahma	4,320,000,000	= 9

$$432 \div 3 = 144$$
9 _____ 9

[12] Because a Maha-Yuga is a one thousands part of one Day of Brahma.

As Brahma's Night is of equal duration, one Day and Night of Brahma would contain	8,640,000,000	= 9
360 of such days and nights make one year of Brahma which is	3,110,400,000,000	= 9
100 such years constitute the whole period of Brahma's age, i.e., Maha-Kalpa	311,040,000,000,000	= 9

311 TRILLION MORTAL years.

"These are the exoteric figures accepted throughout India, and they dovetail pretty nearly with those of the Secret works."[13]

So, 1,955,884,687 years have passed from the moment of the beginning of the evolution on globe **A** of the Earth in the First Round.

However, from all these figures we will need only two. 18,618,728 years have passed from the moment of formation of the physical man. And 308,448,000 years – the period of one minor Manvantara – are necessary for the evolution of the seven races of our fourth round on globe **D**.

Well, now we can set about describing the human races as such starting from the first one.

1887 minus 4989 ⟹ – 3102

2012 minus –3102 ⟹ 5114

times 5 ⟹ 25,570

Last Harvest was

2012 minus 25570 ⟹ 23558 B.C.

---

[13] The Secret Doctrine, Vol. 2, p. 68-70

The First Human Root Race

I n accordance with the Law of Similarity it would be possible to assume that just as any planet of this material universe first exists in the subtle plane and then materialises in the physical plane, gradually becoming more and more dense, exactly the same principles are inherent in the development of man. Primarily the Divine monad exists and then it gradually clothes itself into denser and denser bodies.

"Finally, it is shown in every ancient scripture and Cosmogony that man evolved primarily as a luminous incorporeal form, over which, like the molten brass round the clay model of the sculptor, the physical frame of his body was built by, through, and from, the lower forms and types of animal terrestrial life.

'The Soul and the Form when descending on Earth put on an earthly garment,' says the Zohar."[14]

The authors of *The Secret Doctrine* presented the understanding of how humanity of the First and the following Races developed according to *The Book of Dzyan·* and the Commentaries to it, of which they had an intimate knowledge.

In various ancient teachings, of which *The Bible* is mere a pale reflection, mention is made of the Supreme Spirits, Beings, Dhyana-Cogans and Logoi (they can be called the Supreme Angels if we stick to the terminology of the Teaching of the Ascended Masters), who are "first-begotten" by Brahma – born by Mind. These beings are subdivided into various classes. Now it becomes possible to understand the sense of the stanza from *The Book of Dzyan*, given in *The Secret Doctrine*:

---

[14] The Secret Doctrine, Vol. 2, p. 112

"12. The Great Chohans[15] called the Lords of the Moon, of the Airy Bodies. 'Bring forth Men[16], Men of your nature. Give them[17] their Forms within. She[18] will build Coverings without[19]. Males-Females will they be. Lords of the Flame also...'

"13. They[20] went each on his allotted Land: Seven of them each on his Lot. The Lords of the Flame remain behind. They would not go, they would not create.

"14. The Seven Hosts, the 'Will-born Lords'[21], propelled by the Spirit of Life-giving[22], separate Men from themselves, each on his own Zone[23]."

In accordance with the Law of Cosmic Cycles the time has come for the humanity of this fourth round on planet Earth to emerge. By all appearances, this event could have taken place 200-300 million years ago.

There were beings belonging to the Spirits of the Moon or Pitri, who agreed to create, and there were others, called the Lords of the Flame, who refused. This served as a cause for blaming those angels who abandoned the creation for a rebellion against God.

However these Beings *"devoid of the grosser creative fire, hence unable to create physical man, having no Double, or Astral Body, to project, since they were without any 'form', are shown in exoteric allegories as Yogis, Kumaras (chaste youths), who*

---

[15] The Masters.

[16] It was said to them.

[17] i.e. the Jivas or Monads.

[18] Mother Earth or Nature.

[19] The external Bodies.

[20] The Lords of the Moon

[21] Or Reason-born.

[22] Fohat.

[23] The Secret Doctrine, Vol. 2, p. 17-18

became 'rebels', Asuras, fighting and opposing gods, etc., etc."[24]

It is hard for us to judge what happened in reality. But in some way this event created karma or a condition for the future descending of these Higher Beings into the bodies of the people of the Third Race. But now, lest we should interrupt the narration, we will just bear in mind that in the evolution of angels there were beings too pure and spiritually independent who risked persisting in their opinion and refused to "create".

"Where there is no struggle, there is no merit. Humanity, 'of the Earth earthy', was not destined to be created by the angels of the first divine Breath: therefore they are said to have refused to do so, and man had to be formed by more material creators, who, in their turn, could give only what they had in their own natures, and no more."[25]

The obedient angels projected from their astral bodies their shadows (Chhaya) that became the bodies of the people of the First Race.

"The first race of men were, then, simply the images, the astral doubles, of their Fathers, who were the pioneers, or the most progressed Entities from a preceding though lower sphere, the shell of which is now our Moon."[26]

They were gigantic epicene aeriform beings with the height of 173 feet, or 53 metres (for comparison: the Statue of Liberty in New-York is 105 feet, or 34 metres). These forms knew no death and were leading an unconscious existence similar to a dream during many millions of years.

---

[24] The Secret Doctrine, Vol. 2, p. 78

[25] *Ibid.*, p. 95

[26] *Ibid.*, p. 115

"Therefore the First Root-race of men, sexless and mindless, had to be overthrown and 'hidden until after a time'; i.e., the first race, instead of dying, disappeared in the second race, as certain lower lives and plants do in their progeny. It was a wholesale transformation. The First became the Second Root-race, without either begetting it, procreating it, or dying."[27]

[27] *Ibid.*, p. 84

The Second Root Race

T he second root race appeared by gemmation or transpiration out of the First Race.

"How could these Chhayas reproduce themselves otherwise; viz., procreate the Second Race, since they were ethereal, a-sexual, and even devoid, as yet, of the vehicle of desire, or Kama Rupa, which evolved only in the Third Race? They evolved the Second Race unconsciously, as do some plants. Or, perhaps, as the Amoeba, only on a more ethereal, impressive, and larger scale."[28]

"The old (primitive) Race merged in the second race, and became one with it.

"This is the mysterious process of transformation and evolution of mankind. The material of the first forms – shadowy, ethereal, and negative – was drawn or absorbed into, and thus became the complement of the forms of the Second Race. The Commentary explains this by saying that, as the First Race was simply composed of the astral shadows of the creative progenitors, having of course neither astral nor physical bodies of their own – this Race never died. Its 'men' melted gradually away, becoming absorbed in the bodies of their own 'sweat-born' progeny, more solid than their own. The old form vanished and was absorbed by, disappeared in, the new form, more human and physical. There was no death in those days of a period more blissful than the Golden Age; but the first, or parent material was used for the formation of the new being, to form the body and even

---

28 The Secret Doctrine, Vol. 2, p. 116

the inner or lower principles or bodies of the progeny."[29]

The Second Race was already denser, but it still did not have a physical body. The stature of this Race was 120 feet or about 37 metres.

The Secret Doctrine tells of the habitat of this Race as the second Hyperborean continent. It was situated in the area of the North Pole. Each Race had its continent where it could develop. Only the continent of the First Race is said to continue existing during all the Races of this Manvantara. The continents of the rest of the Races are formed when the Race begins its development and disappear together with the disappearance of the Race. Hence, the continent of the Second Race – the Hyperborean – extinguished together with that Race. A recent investigation in the region of Newfoundland implicitly acknowledges the statements of *The Secret Doctrine*. During the drilling to a depth of over than 1000 metres it was discovered that 55 million years ago (exactly at that time the Second Race must have still existed) in the region of the North Pole the climate was Mediterranean.

"The First Root-Race, the 'Shadows' of the Progenitors, could not be injured, or destroyed by death. Being so ethereal and so little human in constitution, they could not be affected by any element – flood or fire. But their 'Sons', the Second Root-Race, could be and were so destroyed."

"The everblooming lands of the Second Continent (Greenland, among others) were transformed, in order, from Edens with their eternal spring, into hyperborean Hades. This transformation was due to

---

[29] *Ibid.*, p. 121

the displacement of the great waters of the globe, to oceans changing their beds; and the bulk of the Second Race perished in this first great throe of the evolution and consolidation of the globe during the human period."[30]

---

[30] The Secret Doctrine, Vol. 2, p. 138

The beginning of the Third Race

However strange such a method of reproduction may seem, *"The early Third Race, then, is formed from drops of 'sweat', which, after many a transformation, grow into human bodies"[31]*

In fact, various methods of procreation are characteristic of the Third Race.

The Third Race *"itself is separated into three distinct divisions, consisting of men differently procreated. The first two of these are produced by an oviparous method, presumably unknown to modern Natural History. While the early sub-races of the Third Humanity procreated their species by a kind of exudation of moisture or vital fluid, the drops of which coalescing formed an oviform ball – or shall we say egg? – which served as an extraneous vehicle for the generation therein of a foetus and child, the mode of procreation by the later races changed, in its results at all events. The little ones of the earlier races were entirely sexless – shapeless even for all one knows; but those of the later races were born androgynous. It is in the Third Race that the separation of sexes occurred. From being previously a-sexual, Humanity became distinctly hermaphrodite or bi-sexual; and finally the man-bearing eggs began to give birth, gradually and almost imperceptibly in their evolutionary development, first, to Beings in which one sex predominated over the other, and, finally, to distinct men and women."[32]*

This Race reached the stature of 60 feet or 18 metres, and its habitat was the continent Lemuria. But, I

---

[31] *Ibid.*, p. 177
[32] *Ibid.*, p. 132

think we will have another opportunity to speak about this continent.[33]

"To return, however, once more to the history of the Third Race, the 'Sweat-Born', the 'Egg-bearing', and the 'Androgyne'. Almost sexless, in its early beginnings, it became bisexual or androgynous; very gradually of course. The passage from the former to the latter transformation required numberless generations, during which the simple cell that issued from the earliest parent (the two in one), first developed into a bisexual being; and then the cell, becoming a regular egg, gave forth a unisexual creature. The Third-Race-mankind is the most mysterious of all the hitherto developed five Races. The mystery of the 'How' of the generation of the distinct sexes must, of course, be very obscure here, as it is the business of an embryologist and a specialist, the present work giving only faint outlines of the process. But it is evident that the units of the Third Race humanity began to separate in their pre-natal shells, or eggs, and to issue out of them as distinct male and female babes, ages after the appearance of its early progenitors. And, as time rolled on its geological periods, the newly born sub-races began to lose their natal capacities. Toward the end of the fourth sub-race, the babe lost its faculty of walking as soon as liberated from its shell, and by the end of the fifth, mankind was born under the same conditions and by the same identical process as our historical generations. This required, of course, millions of years. The reader has been made acquainted with the

---

[33] See chapter "The Chronology of the Brahmins" in *The Secret Doctrine* (Vol. 2, p. 66) or chapter "Which period of time we are talking about" in this book.

approximate figures, at least of the exoteric calculations.[34]

On the whole the period of existence of the Third Root Race abounds with various events. About 18 million years ago mankind acquired a physical body. This took place in the times of the Third Root Race. Two more events took place in the times of the same Race – the so-called "fall" of humanity and the so-called "fall" of angels. So, now we have finally come to the subject of our interest.

---

[34] The Secret Doctrine, Vol. 2, p. 197

The fall of angels

For any ancient allegory or any symbol there are seven keys in *The Secret Doctrine,* all of which are in the hands of the Highest Initiated. Therefore, I can present only such a conception of the secret of the "fall" which I got myself while simply reading *The Secret Doctrine.* Since everything set forth below may seem extremely unusual, I will merely quote in general, just slightly adding my own understanding of the quotations.

As follows from the preceding narration, man was gradually assuming a shape during millions of years. Approximately 18 million years ago he obtained his physical body. But, as we have already mentioned, the organisation of the human body is sevenfold. Yet, even after the acquisition of the physical body man of the Third Race was still lacking two principles. I do not think I will make a great offence against the truth if I say that these two bodies can be associated with the mental body and the Christ Self according to the terminology of the Teaching of the Ascended Masters. Man did not possess reason, he was a man only in his shape, but, intrinsically, there was no difference between man and animals. Besides, man did not have a mediator that could connect his spiritual part with his physical part.

Stanza VII from *The Book of Dzyan* describes how man gained his Reason.

24. THE SONS OF WISDOM, THE SONS OF NIGHT (*issued from the body of Brahma when it became Night*), READY FOR RE-BIRTH, CAME DOWN. THEY SAW THE (*intellectually*) VILE FORMS OF THE FIRST THIRD (*still senseless Race*)

(a). "WE CAN CHOOSE," SAID THE LORDS (*Masters of Wisdom*), "WE HAVE WISDOM." SOME ENTERED THE CHHAYA (*shadow, image, or astral body*). SOME PROJECTED A SPARK. SOME DEFERRED TILL THE FOURTH (*Race*). FROM THEIR OWN RUPA (essence) THEY FILLED (*intensified*) THE KAMA (*the vehicle of desire*). THOSE WHO ENTERED BECAME ARHATS. THOSE WHO RECEIVED BUT A SPARK REMAINED DESTITUTE OF (*higher*) KNOWLEDGE. THE SPARK BURNT LOW *(b).* THE THIRD REMAINED MIND-LESS. THEIR JIVAS (*Monads*) WERE NOT READY. THESE WERE SET APART AMONG THE SEVEN (*primitive human species*). THEY BECAME NARROW-HEADED. THE THIRD WERE READY. "IN THESE SHALL WE DWELL", SAID THE LORDS OF THE FLAME AND OF THE DARK (*hidden*) WISDOM *(c).*

"This Stanza contains, in itself, the whole key to the mysteries of evil, the so-called Fall of the angels, and the many problems that have puzzled the brains of the philosophers from the time that the memory of man began. It solves the secret of the subsequent inequalities of intellectual capacity, of birth or social position, and gives a logical explanation to the incomprehensible Karmic course throughout the aeons which followed. The best explanation which can be given, in view of the difficulties of the subject, shall now be attempted."[35]

Who were those Sons of Wisdom, who endowed man with Reason? Do you remember those angels who refused "to create"? In different religious systems they have different names. *"All these are the Manasam and*

---

[35] The Secret Doctrine, Vol. 2, p. 161

Rajasas: the Kumaras, Asuras, and other rulers and Pitris, who incarnated in the Third Race, and in this and various other ways endowed mankind with Mind."[36]

"Trans-Himalayan Occultists regard them as evidently identical with those who in India are termed Kumaras, Agnishwattas, and the Barhishads."[37]

"In the Aryan allegory the rebellious Sons of Brahma are all represented as holy ascetics and Yogis. Re-born in every Kalpa, they generally try to impede the work of human procreation."[38]

"There is an eternal cyclic law of re-births, and the series is headed at every new Manvantaric dawn by those who had enjoyed their rest from re-incarnations in previous Kalpas for incalculable Æons – by the highest and the earliest Nirvanees. It was the turn of those 'Gods' to incarnate in the present Manvantara; hence their presence on Earth, and the ensuing allegories; hence, also, the perversion of the original meaning. The Gods who had fallen into generation, whose mission it was to complete divine man, are found represented later on as Demons, evil Spirits, and fiends, at feud and war with Gods, or the irresponsible agents of the one Eternal law. But no conception of such creatures as the devils and Satan of the Christian, Jewish, and Mahomedan religions was ever intended under those thousand and one Aryan allegories."[39]

"The supposed 'rebels,' then, were simply those who, compelled by Karmic law to drink the cup of gall to its last bitter drop, had to incarnate anew, and thus

---

[36] The Secret Doctrine, Vol. 2, p. 89
[37] *Ibid.*, p. 88
[38] *Ibid.*, p. 82
[39] *Ibid.*, p. 232

make responsible thinking entities of the astral statues projected by their inferior brethren. Some are said to have refused, because they had not in them the requisite materials – i.e., an astral body – since they were arupa.[40] The refusal of others had reference to their having been Adepts and Yogis of long past preceding Manvantaras; another mystery. But, later on, as Nirmanakayas[41], they sacrificed themselves for the good and salvation of the Monads which were waiting for their turn, and which otherwise would have had to linger for countless ages in irresponsible, animal-like, though in appearance human, forms. It may be a parable and an allegory within an allegory. Its solution is left to the intuition of the student, if he only reads that which follows with his spiritual eye."[42]

"...the 'first-born' are those who are first set in motion at the beginning of a Manvantara, and thus the first to fall into the lower spheres of materiality. They who are called in Theology 'the Thrones,' and are the 'Seat of God,' must be the first incarnated men on Earth; and it becomes comprehensible, if we think of the endless series of past Manvantaras, to find that the last had to come first, and the first last. We find, in short, that the higher Angels had broken, countless aeons before, through the 'Seven Circles,' and thus robbed them of the Sacred fire; which means in plain words, that they had assimilated during their past incarnations, in lower as well as in higher worlds, all the wisdom therefrom – the reflection of MAHAT in its various degrees of intensity. No Entity, whether angelic or human, can reach the state of Nirvana, or

---

[40] Arupa – not having a form.
[41] Nirmanakaya – the form of that adept or yogi who sacrificed the state of nirvana in order to help humanity.
[42] The Secret Doctrine, Vol. 2, p. 94

of absolute purity, except through aeons of suffering and the knowledge of EVIL as well as of good, as otherwise the latter remains incomprehensible.

"Between man and the animal – whose Monads (or Jivas) are fundamentally identical – there is the impassable abyss of Mentality and Self-consciousness. What is human mind in its higher aspect, whence comes it, if it is not a portion of the essence – and, in some rare cases of incarnation, the very essence – of a higher Being: one from a higher and divine plane?"[43]

As we see, humanity got for its further development the Christ Selves which were not the worst ones. And since *"the mankind of the First Root-Race is the mankind of the second, third, fourth, fifth, etc., to the last it forms a cyclic and constant reincarnation of the Monads belonging to the Dhyan Chohans of our Planetary chain,"[44]* then as a matter of fact, these Christ Selves that were obtained during the Third Root Race are the very Christ Selves which we possess, our guardian angels, our Logi, which the Christian doctrine called fallen angels so vigorously.

"The fallen Angels are made in every ancient system the prototypes of fallen men – allegorically, and, those men themselves – esoterically."[45]

Now let's try to understand the mechanism with the help of which we obtained our Reason.

There were three classes of the Masters of Wisdom. Some of them entered the Chhaya, others projected a spark, and the rest deferred till the Fourth Race.

---

[43] The Secret Doctrine, Vol. 2, p. 80-81

[44] *Ibid.*, p. 146, footnote.

[45] *Ibid.*, p. 390

So, a part of the Higher Beings descended into the people's bodies.

"The power, by which they first created, is just that which has since caused them to be degraded from their high status to the position of evil spirits, of Satan and his Host, created in their turn by the unclean fancy of exoteric creeds. It was by Kriyasakti, that mysterious and divine power latent in the will of every man, and which, if not called to life, quickened and developed by Yogi-training, remains dormant in 999,999 men out of a million, and gets atrophied. This power is explained in the 'Twelve Signs of the Zodiac'[46], as follows:–

'Kriyasakti – the mysterious power of thought which enables it to produce external, perceptible, phenomenal results by its own inherent energy. The ancients held that any idea will manifest itself externally, if one's attention (and Will) is deeply concentrated upon it; similarly, an intense volition will be followed by the desired result. A Yogi generally performs his wonders by means of Itchasakti (Will-power) and Kriyasakti.'

"The Third Race had thus created the so-called SONS OF WILL AND YOGA, or the 'ancestors' (the spiritual forefathers) of all the subsequent and present Arhats, or Mahatmas, in a truly immaculate way. They were indeed created, not begotten, as were their brethren of the Fourth Race, who were generated sexually after the separation of sexes, the Fall of Man. For creation is but the result of will acting on phenomenal matter, the calling forth out of it the primordial divine Light and eternal Life. They were

[46] See "Five Years of Theosophy," p. 777 (The footnote is copied from the book *The Secret Doctrine*)

the 'holy seed-grain' of the future Saviours of Humanity."[47]

"We now come to an important point with regard to the double evolution of the human race. The Sons of Wisdom, or the spiritual Dhyanis, had become 'intellectual' through their contact with matter, because they had already reached, during previous cycles of incarnation, that degree of intellect which enabled them to become independent and self-conscious entities, on this plane of matter. They were reborn only by reason of Karmic effects. They entered those who were 'ready', and became the Arhats, or sages, alluded to above. This needs explanation.

"It does not mean that Monads entered forms in which other Monads already were. They were 'Essences', 'Intelligences', and conscious spirits; entities seeking to become still more conscious by uniting with more developed matter. Their essence was too pure to be distinct from the universal essence; but their 'Egos', or Manas (since they are called Manasaputra, born of 'Mahat', or Brahma) had to pass through earthly human experiences to become all-wise, and be able to start on the returning ascending cycle. The Monads are not discrete principles, limited or conditioned, but rays from that one universal absolute Principle. The entrance into a dark room through the same aperture of one ray of sunlight following another will not constitute two rays, but one ray intensified."[48]

So, here you have an explanation of the fact that when a human is "ready", there can be one or several

---

[47] The Secret Doctrine, Vol. 2, p. 173
[48] *Ibid.*, p. 167

Higher Beings present in this human being with the purpose of carrying out a certain mission.

"Thus, those who were 'half ready,' who received 'but a spark,' constitute the average humanity which has to acquire its intellectuality during the present Manvantaric evolution, after which they will be ready in the next for the full reception of the 'Sons of Wisdom'. While those which 'were not ready' at all, the latest Monads, which had hardly evolved from their last transitional and lower animal forms at the close of the Third Round, remained the 'narrow-brained'[49] of the Stanza. This explains the otherwise unaccountable degrees of intellectuality among the various races of men – the savage Bushman and the European – even now."[50]

Narrow headed, deprived of reason, but already separated into two genders, human beings originally could not direct their sexual instinct properly and began to copulate with she-animals. All the modern species of monkeys are a by-product of such combinations, as *The Secret Doctrine* teaches. This begot karma which devolved upon those Sons of Wisdom who deferred till the Fourth Race.

"It is only after the so-called FALL, that the races began to develop rapidly into a purely human shape. And, in order that a student may correctly comprehend the full meaning of the Fall, so mystic and transcendental is it in its real significance, he

---

[49] The term here means neither the dolicho-cephalic nor the brachyo-cephalic, nor yet skulls of a smaller volume, but simply brains devoid of intellect generally. (The footnote is copied from the book *The Secret Doctrine*)

[50] The Secret Doctrine, Vol. 2, p. 168

must be told at once the details which preceded this event; of which event modern theology has formed a pivot on which its most pernicious and absurd dogmas and beliefs are made to turn.

"The archaic commentaries explain, as the reader must remember, that, of the Host of Dhyanis, whose turn it was to incarnate as the Egos of the immortal, but, on this plane, senseless monads – that some 'obeyed' (the law of evolution) immediately when the men of the Third Race became physiologically and physically ready, i.e., when they had separated into sexes. These were those early conscious Beings who, now adding conscious knowledge and will to their inherent Divine purity, created by Kriyasakti the semi-Divine man, who became the seed on earth for future adepts. Those, on the other hand, who, jealous of their intellectual freedom (unfettered as it then was by the bonds of matter), said:– 'We can choose... we have wisdom', and incarnated far later – these had their first Karmic punishment prepared for them. They got bodies (physiologically) inferior to their astral models, because their chhayas had belonged to progenitors of an inferior degree in the seven classes. As to those 'Sons of Wisdom' who had 'deferred' their incarnation till the Fourth Race, which was already tainted (physiologically) with sin and impurity, they produced a terrible cause, the Karmic result of which weighs on them to this day. It was produced in themselves, and they became the carriers of that seed of iniquity for aeons to come, because the bodies they had to inform had become defiled through their own procrastination.

"This was the 'Fall of the angels,' because of their rebellion against Karmic Law."[51]

---

[51] The Secret Doctrine, Vol. 2, p. 227-228

And a few more excerpts in conclusion.

"...not all men became incarnations of the 'divine Rebels,' but only a few among them. The remainder had their fifth principle simply quickened by the spark thrown into it, which accounts for the great difference between the intellectual capacities of men and races. Had not the 'sons of Mahat,' speaking allegorically, skipped the intermediate worlds, in their impulse toward intellectual freedom, the animal man would never have been able to reach upward from this earth, and attain through self-exertion his ultimate goal. The cyclic pilgrimage would have to be performed through all the planes of existence half unconsciously, if not entirely so, as in the case of the animals. It is owing to this rebellion of intellectual life against the morbid inactivity of pure spirit, that we are what we are – self-conscious, thinking men, with the capabilities and attributes of Gods in us, for good as much as for evil. Hence the REBELS are our saviours. Let the philosopher ponder well over this, and more than one mystery will become clear to him. It is only by the attractive force of the contrasts that the two opposites – Spirit and Matter – can be cemented on Earth, and, smelted in the fire of selfconscious experience and suffering, find themselves wedded in Eternity. This will reveal the meaning of many hitherto incomprehensible allegories, foolishly called 'fables'."[52]

"...it is owing to the Radiant Archangels, Dhyans-Chohans, who refused to create, because they wanted Man to become his own creator and an immortal god – that men can reach Nirvana and the haven of heavenly divine Peace.

---

[52] *Ibid.*, p. 103

"To close this rather lengthy comment, the Secret Doctrine teaches that the Fire-Devas, the Rudras, and the Kumaras, the 'Virgin-Angels,' (to whom Michael and Gabriel, the Archangels, both belong), the divine 'Rebels'... preferred the curse of incarnation and the long cycles of terrestrial existence and rebirths, to seeing the misery (even if unconscious) of the beings (evolved as shadows out of their Brethren) through the semi-passive energy of their too spiritual Creators. If 'man's uses of life should be such as neither to animalize nor to spiritualize, but to humanize Self,' before he can do so, he must be born human not angelic. Hence, tradition shows the celestial Yogis offering themselves as voluntary victims in order to redeem Humanity – created god-like and perfect at first – and to endow him with human affections and aspirations. To do this they had to give up their natural status and, descending on our globe, take up their abode on it for the whole cycle of the Mahayuga, thus exchanging their impersonal individualities for individual personalities – the bliss of sidereal existence for the curse of terrestrial life. This voluntary sacrifice of the Fiery Angels, whose nature was Knowledge and Love, was construed by the exoteric theologies into a statement that shows 'the rebel angels hurled down from heaven into the darkness of Hell' – our Earth."[53]

"...there never were any devils or 'disobedient Angels,' for the simple reason that they are all governed by Law."[54]

"The 'Fallen Angels,' so-called, are Humanity itself. The Demon of Pride, Lust, Rebellion, and Hatred, has never had any being before the

---

[53] The Secret Doctrine, Vol. 2, p. 246

[54] *Ibid.*, p. 487

appearance of physical conscious man. It is man who has begotten, nurtured, and allowed the fiend to develop in his heart; he, again, who has contaminated the indwelling god in himself, by linking the pure spirit with the impure demon of matter."[55]

1) So what about Battle between Archangels Michael vs Lucifer?

2) What about Archangel Lucifer going thru the 2nd Death in 1975?

---

[55] *Ibid.*, p. 274

The fall of humanity

"Meanwhile, one task is left incomplete: that of disposing of that most pernicious of all the theological dogmas – the CURSE under which mankind is alleged to have suffered ever since the supposed disobedience of Adam and Eve in the bower of Eden."[56]

The description contained in the Bible, according to *The Secret Doctrine*, was borrowed by the Israelites from more ancient sources, in particular from the Chaldeans. Let's remember what is said in the Bible about the Fall of Adam and Eve.

The serpent... said to the woman, "Did God really say, 'You must not eat from any tree in the garden'?" The woman said to the serpent, "We may eat fruit from the trees in the garden, but God did say, 'You must not eat fruit from the tree that is in the middle of the garden, and you must not touch it, or you will die'". "You will not surely die," the serpent said to the woman. "For God knows that when you eat of it your eyes will be opened, and you will be like God, knowing good and evil." When the woman saw that the fruit of the tree was good for food and pleasing to the eye, and also desirable for gaining wisdom, she took some and ate it. She also gave some to her husband, who was with her, and he ate it. Then the eyes of both of them were opened, and they realized they were naked; so they sewed fig leaves together and made coverings for themselves.[57]

---

[56] The Secret Doctrine, Vol. 2, p. 410
[57] Genesis 3:1-7. Here and further the passages from the Gospel are marked in **bold** font.

The Secret Doctrine says, **"The 'tree' is man himself, of course, and the Serpents dwelling in each, the conscious Manas, the connecting link between Spirit and Matter, heaven and earth."**[58]

"The Fall was the result of man's knowledge, for his 'eyes were opened'. Indeed, he was taught Wisdom and the hidden knowledge by the 'Fallen Angel', for the latter had become from that day his Manas, Mind and Self-consciousness."[59]

"...and the expression of the allegorical serpent does not... refer at all to the physiological fall of men, but to their acquiring the knowledge of good and evil, which knowledge comes to them prior to their fall. It must not be forgotten that it is only after his forced expulsion from Eden that 'Adam knew Eve his wife'".[60]

For some reason the jealous Elohim and gods – the inhabitants of Paradise – did not want man to become one of them. I could not understand for a long time what gods they could be that did not want the brainchild they had created themselves – man – to develop. As always, "by chance", *The Apocryphon of John*, a disciple of Jesus, in which the essence of what happened was explained, came to my hand. Since this apocryphon was written by a disciple of Jesus, it becomes clear that the knowledge Jesus was giving his disciples did not differ from the teaching of *The Secret Doctrine*. And it could not have been otherwise, as Jesus was an Initiated. It is true that later on the essence was completely withdrawn from these teachings and many things in the interpretation of the church fathers

---

[58] The Secret Doctrine, Vol. 2, p. 98

[59] *Ibid.*, p. 513

[60] *Ibid.*, p. 279

acquired a diametrically opposed meaning. Later on we will have an opportunity to get acquainted with this apocryphon. But in the interim I will continue the explanation of *The Secret Doctrine* concerning the "fall" of man.

So, man acquired reason. The fire of Reason. Intellect. Knowledge. However, any of these qualities can be used both for good and for evil.

"Great intellect and too much knowledge are a two-edged weapon in life, and instruments for evil as well as for good. When combined with Selfishness, they will make of the whole of Humanity a footstool for the elevation of him who possesses them, and a means for the attainment of his objects; while, applied to altruistic humanitarian purposes, they may become the means of the salvation of many. At all events, the absence of selfconsciousness and intellect will make of man an idiot, a brute in human form."[61]

By itself the possession of Reason obliges man to consciously make a choice between Good and Evil. Now he can choose. Reason in man, at bottom, is his initiator. And, using this tool, man can either really become a co-creator of God or use his Reason in order to achieve any illusory goals in this world.

The same creative fire is used by man for procreating offspring, now already sexually.

"The separation of the sexes was in the programme of nature and of natural evolution; and the creative faculty in male and female was a gift of Divine wisdom."[62]

---

[61] The Secret Doctrine, Vol. 2, p. 163
[62] *Ibid.*, p. 217

The beginning of sexual intimacy between man and woman was not a sin. This is a myth. However, in our dual world this ability was perverted as well, which already really was and is a sin. I will cite a long passage from *The Secret Doctrine*, as I would be unable to say it better than it was said there.

"Creative powers in man were the gift of divine wisdom, not the result of sin. This is clearly instanced in the paradoxical behaviour of Jehovah, who first curses Adam and Eve (or Humanity) for the supposed committed crime, and then blesses his 'chosen people' by saying 'Be fruitful and multiply, and replenish the earth' (Gen. ix. 1). The curse was not brought on mankind by the Fourth Race, for the comparatively sinless Third Race, the still more gigantic Antediluvians, had perished in the same way; hence the Deluge was no punishment, but simply a result of a periodical and geological law. Nor was the curse of KARMA called down upon them for seeking natural union, as all the mindless animal-world does in its proper seasons; but, for abusing the creative power, for desecrating the divine gift, and wasting the life-essence for no purpose except bestial personal gratification. When understood, the third chapter of Genesis will be found to refer to the Adam and Eve of the closing Third and the commencing Fourth Races. In the beginning, conception was as easy for woman as it was for all animal creation. Nature had never intended that woman should bring forth her young ones 'in sorrow.' Since that period, however, during the evolution of the Fourth Race, there came enmity between its seed, and the 'Serpent's' seed, the seed or product of Karma and divine wisdom. For the seed of woman or lust, bruised the head of the seed of the

fruit of wisdom and knowledge, by turning the holy mystery of procreation into animal gratification; hence the law of Karma 'bruised the heel' of the Atlantean race, by gradually changing physiologically, morally, physically, and mentally, the whole nature of the Fourth Race of mankind[63], until, from the healthy King of animal creation of the Third Race, man became in the Fifth, our race, a helpless, scrofulous being, and has now become the wealthiest heir on the globe to constitutional and hereditary diseases, the most consciously and intelligently bestial of all animals![64]

"This is the real CURSE from the physiological standpoint, almost the only one touched upon in the Kabalistic esotericism. Viewed from this aspect, the curse is undeniable, for it is evident."[65]

Having obtained Reason, humanity has to constantly be in a state of struggle, which is taking place within it and naturally has an impact on the surrounding world. We have to burn in the fire of passion, desires, being motivated by illusion and

---

[63] How wise and grand, how far-seeing and morally beneficent are the laws of Manu on connubial life, when compared with the licence tacitly allowed to man in civilized countries. That those laws have been neglected for the last two millenniums does not prevent us from admiring their forethought. The Brahmin was a grihasta, a family man, till a certain period of his life, when, after begetting a son, he broke with married life and became a chaste Yogi. His very connubial life was regulated by his Brahmin astrologer in accordance with his nature. Therefore, in such countries as the Punjab, for instance, where the lethal influence of Mussulman, and later on of European, licentiousness, has hardly touched the orthodox Aryan castes, one still finds the finest men — so far as stature and physical strength go — on the whole globe; whereas the mighty men of old have found themselves replaced in the Deccan, and especially in Bengal, by men whose generation becomes with every century (and almost with every year) dwarfed and weakened.

[64] Diseases and over-population are facts that can never be denied.

[65] The Secret Doctrine, Vol. 2, p. 410-411

plunging into this illusion deeper and deeper. The created karma leads to suffering, and suffering makes us change and remember God and follow His Law.

"This war will last till the inner and divine man adjusts his outer terrestrial self to his own spiritual nature. Till then the dark and fierce passions of the former will be at eternal feud with his master, the Divine Man. But the animal will be tamed one day, because its nature will be changed, and harmony will reign once more between the two as before the 'Fall', when even mortal man was created by the Elements and was not born."[66]

In conclusion of this chapter I would like to mention a description of one Chaldean image from the British Museum given in *The Secret Doctrine*:

"Representing the events of the Fall... there are also two figures sitting on each side of a tree, and holding out their hands to the 'apple', while at the back of the 'Tree' is the Dragon-Serpent. Esoterically, the two figures are two 'Chaldees'[67] ready for initiation, the Serpent symbolising the 'Initiator'; while the jealous gods, who curse the three, are the exoteric profane clergy. Not much of the literal 'Biblical event' there, as any occultist can see."[68]

---

[66] *Ibid.*, p. 268
[67] Chaldees or Chaldeans – at first a tribe, then a cast of scientists-cabbalists. They were scientists, magicians of Babylon, astrologists and soothsayers.
[68] The Secret Doctrine, Vol. 2, p. 354

The origin of evil

I am not going to present in a few pages a full treatment of the viewpoint of *The Secret Doctrine* on the origin of Evil. But I will try to present some of my understanding.

"The ABSOLUTE is not to be defined, and no mortal or immortal has ever seen or comprehended it during the periods of Existence. The mutable cannot know the Immutable, nor can that which lives perceive Absolute Life."[69] – states *The Secret Doctrine.*

However, something prompts the One to create, to father. *"Creation is shown as a sport, an amusement (Lila) of the creative god. The Zohar speaks of primordial worlds, which perished as soon as they came into existence."* *"In the Hindu Puranas, Brahma, the creator, is seen recommencing de novo several creations after as many failures..."*[70]

And this relates to the universe, to the worlds and to our Earth. I also asked myself what makes God create. In one of the meditations I was given an image. God is like a child sitting on the shore of the ocean and building a sand castle. Over night the ocean destroys this creation, and in the morning he comes to the shore of the ocean again and builds his sand castle anew. Why does a child do it? Perhaps, God does it for the same reason.

So, at first a thought appears, a motive for the beginning of the creation. And this very thought itself already has a state opposite to the ABSOLUTE. In this very thought a duality is already contained.

---

[69] The Secret Doctrine, Vol. 2, p. 34
[70] *Ibid.*, p. 53

"The esoteric meaning of the word Logos (speech or word, Verbum) is the rendering in objective expression, as in a photograph, of the concealed thought. The Logos is the mirror reflecting DIVINE MIND, and the Universe is the mirror of the Logos, though the latter is the esse of that Universe. As the Logos reflects all in the Universe of Pleroma, so man reflects in himself all that he sees and finds in his Universe, the Earth."[71]

"There was no 'EVIL thought' that originated the opposing Power, but simply THOUGHT per se; something which, being cogitative, and containing design and purpose, is therefore finite, and must thus find itself naturally in opposition to pure quiescence, the as natural state of absolute Spirituality and Perfection. It was simply the law of Evolution that asserted itself; the progress of mental unfolding, differentiated from spirit, involved and entangled already with matter, into which it is irresistibly drawn. Ideas, in their very nature and essence, as conceptions bearing relation to objects, whether true or imaginary, are opposed to absolute THOUGHT, that unknowable ALL..."[72]

" 'Every Universe (world or planet) has its own Logos,' says the doctrine. The Sun was always called by the Egyptians 'the eye of Osiris,' and was himself the Logos, the first-begotten, or light made manifest to the world, 'which is the Mind and divine intellect of the Concealed.' It is only by the sevenfold Ray of this light that we can become cognizant of the Logos through the Demiurge, regarding the latter as the

---

[71] *Ibid.*, p. 25
[72] *Ibid.*, p. 490

creator of our planet and everything pertaining to it, and the former as the guiding Force of that 'Creator' – good and bad at the same time, the origin of good and the origin of evil. This 'Creator' is neither good nor bad per se, but its differentiated aspects in nature make it assume one or the other character."[73]

"…Logos manifesting itself as a double principle of Good and Evil."[74]

"To those who, prompted by old theological prejudice, may say: 'But the Asuras are the rebel Devas, the opponents of the Gods – hence devils, and the spirits of Evil,' it is answered: Esoteric philosophy admits neither good nor evil per se, as existing independently in nature. The cause for both is found, as regards the Kosmos, in the necessity of contraries or contrasts, and with respect to man, in his human nature, his ignorance and passions. There is no devil or the utterly depraved, as there are no Angels absolutely perfect, though there may be spirits of Light and of Darkness…"[75]

"There is no Devil, no Evil, outside mankind to produce a Devil. Evil is a necessity in, and one of the supporters of the manifested universe. It is a necessity for progress and evolution, as night is necessary for the production of Day, and Death for that of Life – that man may live for ever."[76]

EVIL — VEIL: IDENTIFICATION WITH FORM / hence FINITE-NESS
GOOD - GOD: IDENTIFICATION WITH FORMMAKER HENCE INFINITY

[73] The Secret Doctrine, Vol. 2, p. 25
[74] Ibid., p. 214
[75] Ibid., p. 162
[76] Ibid., p. 389

TRUE I.D. IS ID FORM MAKER
THERE IS ONLY THE ETERNAL,
INFINITE ONE, PERFECT
CREATOR.

"Perfection, to be fully such, must be born out of imperfection, the incorruptible must grow out of the corruptible, having the latter as its vehicle and basis and contrast. Absolute light is absolute darkness, and vice versa. In fact, there is neither light nor darkness in the realms of truth. Good and Evil are twins, the progeny of Space and Time, under the sway of Maya. Separate them, by cutting off one from the other, and they will both die. Neither exists per se, since each has to be generated and created out of the other, in order to come into being; both must be known and appreciated before becoming objects of perception, hence, in mortal mind, they must be divided."[77]

"The legend of the 'Fallen Angels' in its esoteric signification, contains the key to the manifold contradictions of human character; it points to the secret of man's self-consciousness; it is the angle-iron on which hinges his entire life-cycle; – the history of his evolution and growth.

"On a firm grasp of this doctrine depends the correct understanding of esoteric anthropogenesis. It gives a clue to the vexed question of the Origin of Evil; and shows how man himself is the separator of the ONE into various contrasted aspects."[78]

"Were it light alone, inactive and absolute, the human mind could not appreciate nor even realise it. Shadow is that which enables light to manifest itself, and gives it objective reality. Therefore, shadow is not evil, but is the necessary and indispensable corollary which completes Light or Good: it is its creator on Earth.

---

[77] *Ibid.*, p. 96
[78] *Ibid.*, p. 274

"According to the views of the Gnostics, these two principles are immutable Light and Shadow, Good and Evil being virtually one and having existed through all eternity, as they will ever continue to exist so long as there are manifested worlds."[79]

FINITE FORMS

In the process of expanding the universe becomes denser and denser and, consequently, becomes more and more different from the natural state of the ABSOLUTE, and finally reaches the maximal point of materiality in which we are now. And if at the start the centrifugal forces predominated for the Spirit and centripetal forces for the Matter, then after the lower turning point the nature of these forces alters: *"viz. matter will become centrifugal and spirit centripetal"*[80].

When man prevails his animal nature, when he allows the Spirit to hold sway over himself, he becomes a co-creator with God, and Spirit, residing within him, aspires insuperably toward its Source, and the worlds contract.

We return to the One, to that place where there is no Evil. VEIL FROM ONE'S TRUE IDENTITY.

---

[79] The Secret Doctrine, Vol. 2, p. 214
[80] *Ibid.*, p. 261

Lucifer

"...ignorance is death, and knowledge alone gives immortality".[81]

T he subject of Good and Evil will be incomplete if we do not mention Lucifer. Perhaps, it will come like a thunder for many, if not for all the readers, that *The Secret Doctrine* does not make of Lucifer a seat of Evil and the person against whom we must fight together with the whole world. I will make an attempt to expand on the topic as far as I understand it.

In every ancient Pantheon dual properties were attributed to the chief-God of that Pantheon. Osiris of the Egyptians, Zeus of the Greeks. Evidently, all these ancient beliefs had one general and far more ancient source. The names changed, but the main events, handed down as legends, remained unaltered.

Ahura Mazda of the Zoroastrians – ancient Persians – had his enemy Ahriman or Angra Mainyu as his antithesis, dark side. In one of the dictations received by Elizabeth Prophet it is pointed out clearly that Ahura Mazda is identical to Sanat Kumara[82].

Exactly in the same way Satan, Devil, Lucifer represent the shadow side of the Deity residing in incarnation.

Ahura Mazda was the chief and the synthesis of the seven Amesha Spentas who can be compared to the seven Spherots of the cabbalists or the seven Kumaras of India.

---

[81] *Ibid.*, p. 215
[82] Beloved Zarathustra. The Class of the Archangels. "God Has Sent the Seven Archangels for the Rescue of the People of Light on Earth"// Pearls of Wisdom. – vol. 24 – http://www.tsl.org.

In a literal translation Ahura Mazda means the Master of Wisdom. And the seven Amesha Spentas or seven Kumaras, Elohim, the seven inspiring gods of Egypt, Chaldea and other countries are the Masters who endowed humanity with Reason. Collectively humanity is their Logos or Son.

And the characteristic attributes of these higher Beings are embodied in each of our principles.

Thus, the Masters of Wisdom are residing in humanity, they have to incarnate in the human bodies over again.

"Once landed on, and having touched this planet of dense matter, no snow-white wings of the highest angel can remain immaculate, or the Avatar (or incarnation) be perfect, as every such Avatar is the fall of a God into generation."[83]

"The Zohar gives it very suggestively. When the 'Holy One' (the Logos) desired to create man, he called the highest host of Angels and said to them what he wanted, but they doubted the wisdom of this desire and answered: 'Man will not continue one night in his glory' – for which they were burnt (annihilated?), by the 'Holy' Lord. Then he called another, lower Host, and said the same. And they contradicted the 'Holy One': 'What is the good of Man?' they argued. Still Elohim created man, and when man sinned there came the hosts of Uzza and Azael, and twitted God: 'Here is the Son of Man that thou hast made,' they said. 'Behold, he sinned!' Then the Holy One replied: 'If you had been among them (men) you would have been worse than they.' And he threw them from their exalted position in Heaven even down on the Earth; and 'they were changed (into

---

[83] The Secret Doctrine, Vol. 2, p. 483

*men) and sinned after the women of the earth';
(Zohar, 9, b.). This is quite plain. No mention is made
in Genesis of these 'Sons of God' (chap. vi.) having
been punished for it. The only reference to it in the
Bible is in Jude (6). 'And the angels which kept not
their first estate but left their habitation, he hath
reserved in everlasting chains under darkness unto
the judgment of the great day.' And this means simply
that the 'Angels,' doomed to incarnation, are in the
chains of flesh and matter, under the darkness of
ignorance, till the 'Great Day,' which will come as
always after the seventh round, after the expiration of
the 'Week,' on the SEVENTH SABBATH, or in the
post-Manvantaric Nirvana."[84]*

*"...because through, and in, the human form they
will become progressive beings, whereas the nature of
the angel is purely intransitive, therefore man has in
him the potency of transcending the faculties of the
Angels."[85]*

*"Thus the god is blended in man, and the man is
deified into a god."[86]*

*"...Paul repeated it in Corinthians I, vi., 3: 'Know
ye not that we (the Initiates) shall judge angels?'"[87]*

*"...thus LUCIFER – the spirit of Intellectual
Enlightenment and Freedom of Thought – is
metaphorically the guiding beacon, which helps man
to find his way through the rocks and sandbanks of
Life, for Lucifer is the LOGOS in his highest, and the*

---

[84] *Ibid.*, p. 490
[85] *Ibid.*, p. 111
[86] The Theosophical Glossary by H.P. Blavatsky
[87] The Secret Doctrine, Vol. 2, p. 111

'Adversary' in his lowest aspect – both of which are reflected in our Ego."[88]

The case with Lucifer is very demonstrational. This is a clear evidence of how the dogma spread by the church fathers has completely distorted the essence of the original event. Lucifer, the Son of Dawn, a Radiant Angel, who endowed humanity with Reason, was degraded to the state of a horned scapegoat, to whom generations of Christians pointed as to the main originator of all the misfortunes and woes on this planet. However, this was and still is the lot of all the Lightbearers. The example with Lucifer is even more demonstrational because his name is translated from Latin exactly as *Lightbearer*.

And even more remarkable is that this metamorphose took place at an utterly recent, historically depicted age. Even in the early Christian times one of the Rome Popes chose for himself the name Lucifer. And in the fourth century there existed a Christian sect, the members of which were called Luciferians. Jesus Himself said **"I, Jesus... am the root... and the bright and Morning Star"**[89] or Lucifer.

In truth humanity resembles "Ivan who neglected his homeland and roots"[90]. It is still residing in the phase of a deep sleep. But "the Sleep of Reason Produces Monsters" like the Devil or Satan.

In order to awake the historical memory and revive the consciousness of those who are able to perceive the Truth, I will give a few more facts and quotations and leave them without comments.

---

[88] The Secret Doctrine, Vol. 2, p. 162
[89] Rev. St. John 22.16
[90] A Russian proverb. (Translator's footnote)

We remember from the foregoing narration that the Masters of Wisdom descended into those representatives of humanity of the Third Race who were ready.

"Alone a handful of primitive men – in whom the spark of divine Wisdom burnt bright, and only strengthened in its intensity as it got dimmer and dimmer with every age in those who turned it to bad purposes – remained the elect custodians of the Mysteries revealed to mankind by the divine Teachers. There were those among them, who remained in their Kumaric condition from the beginning; and tradition whispers, what the secret teachings affirm, namely, that these Elect were the germ of a Hierarchy which never died since that period:–

'The inner man of the first only changes his body from time to time; he is ever the same, knowing neither rest nor Nirvana, spurning Devachan and remaining constantly on Earth for the salvation of mankind... Out of the seven virgin-men (Kumara) four sacrificed themselves for the sins of the world and the instruction of the ignorant, to remain till the end of the present Manvantara. Though unseen, they are ever present. When people say of one of them, 'He is dead'; behold, he is alive and under another form. These are the Head, the Heart, the Soul, and the Seed of undying knowledge (Gnyana). Thou shalt never speak, O Lanoo, of these great ones (Maha...) before a multitude, mentioning them by their names. The wise alone will understand.' **(Catechism of the inner Schools.)**"[91]

However, in another place Blavatsky mentions the names of these seven Saint Kumaras. They are Sanaka,

---

[91] The Secret Doctrine, Vol. 2, p. 281

Sananda, Sanatana, Sanatkumara, Jata, Vodhu and Panchasikha[92].

Lucifer is a Latin name of the planet Venus. According to *The Secret Doctrine,* each of the seven human Races receives its light and life from a certain planet. The Third Race was born under Mars and Venus[93].

"Every active power or force of the earth comes to her from one of the seven Lords. Light comes through Sukra (Venus), who receives a triple supply, and gives one-third of it to the Earth. Therefore the two are called 'Twin-sisters', but the Spirit of the Earth is subservient to the 'Lord' of Sukra."[94]

"Pythagoras calls Sukra-Venus the Sol alter, 'the other Sun.' Of the 'seven palaces of the Sun,' that of Lucifer Venus is the third one in Christian and Jewish Kabala, the Zohar making of it the abode of Samael. (*The Secret Doctrine* identifies Samael with Satan and the Devil – note by T.M.) *According to the Occult Doctrine, this planet is our Earth's primary, and its spiritual prototype."*

"Every sin committed on Earth is felt by Usanas-Sukra... Every change on Sukra is felt on, and reflected by, the Earth."[95]

"It is owing to the fanciful interpretation of the archaic tradition, which states that Venus changes simultaneously (geologically) with the Earth; that whatever takes place on the one takes place on the

---

[92] The Secret Doctrine, Vol. 2, p. 319
[93] *Ibid.,* p. 29
[94] *Ibid.,* p. 29
[95] *Ibid.,* p. 31

other; and that many and great were their common changes – it is for these reasons that St. Augustine repeats it, applying the several changes of configuration, colour, and even of the orbital paths, to that theologically-woven character of Venus-Lucifer."

"As Venus has no satellites, it is stated allegorically, that 'Asphujit' (this 'planet') adopted the Earth, the progeny of the Moon, 'who overgrew its parent and gave much trouble,' a reference to the occult connection between the two. The Regent (of the planet) Sukra[96] loved his adopted child so well that he incarnated as Usanas and gave it perfect laws, which were disregarded and rejected in later ages."[97]

"Venus, or Lucifer (also Sukra and Usanas) the planet, is the light-bearer of our Earth, in both its physical and mystic sense. The Christians knew it well in early times, since one of the earliest popes of Rome is known by his Pontiff name as Lucifer."[98]

"But in antiquity and reality, Lucifer, or Luciferus, is the name of the angelic Entity presiding over the light of truth as over the light of the day. In the great Valentinian gospel Pistis Sophia it is taught that of the three Powers emanating from the Holy names of the Three (Τριδσνάμεις), that of Sophia (the Holy Ghost according to these gnostics – the most cultured of all), resides in the planet Venus or Lucifer."[99]

---

[96] Sukra is the son of Bhrigu the great Rishi, and one of the Seven Prajapati, the founder of the Race of Bhargavas, in which Parasu Rama is born. (The footnote from The Secret Doctrine, p. 32.)

[97] The Secret Doctrine, Vol. 2, p. 31

[98] *Ibid.*, p. 33

[99] *Ibid.*, p. 512

"And now it stands proven that Satan, or the Red Fiery Dragon... and Lucifer, or 'Light-Bearer,' is in us: it is our Mind – our tempter and Redeemer, our intelligent liberator and Saviour from pure animalism. Without this principle – the emanation of the very essence of the pure divine principle Mahat (Intelligence), which radiates direct from the Divine mind – we would be surely no better than animals." [100]

---

[100] The Secret Doctrine, Vol. 2, p. 513

A short digression

As soon as we have started to talk about the connection of planet Venus and Lucifer with the Earth, I cannot help quoting the second dictation of Sanat Kumara "The Dispensation* Granted" from the series "The Opening of the Seventh Seal"[101] received by the messenger Elizabeth Clare Prophet in the year 1979. The story, antecedent to the embodiment on Earth of the Master of planet Venus, is just told in this dictation. Besides, it is always interesting to watch how one and the same event is reproduced in different sources and how the Truth is refracted through the consciousness of the Messengers of the Hierarchy. In general, *The Secret Doctrine* mostly deals with the comparison of how one and the same truth is given in various sources. So, let us follow the tradition.

---

* Dispensation – God's grace
[101] Pearls of Wisdom, Vol. 1 – http://www.tsl.org

The opening of the seventh seal

II The Dispensation Granted

A nd I saw a great white throne and him that sat on it, from whose face the earth and the heaven fled away; and there was found no place for them.

I am Alpha and Omega, the beginning and the ending, saith the Lord, which is, and which was, and which is to come, the Almighty.

Revelation 20:11; 1:8

Souls of the Saints Robed in White:

I come from the great white throne, the I AM THAT I AM in the person of the Ancient of Days. In the name of the Father, of the Son, and of the Holy Ghost, I sit upon the seat of authority. I AM he from whose face the earth and the heaven shall flee away, and there shall no place be found for the seed of the wicked. AUM.

My heart is the heart of the Trinity. My heart is the heart of God. Through my heart there flows from the One the pure river of water of life, clear as crystal, proceeding out of the throne of God and of the Lamb which is the foundation of worlds above and below. Lo, I AM the Alpha and the Omega of that water of life. I AM the emissary of the plus and the minus of the perpetual flow of the dayspring from on high.

This is the water of the Lamb descending from the Universal Source heart to heart to heart. And unto him that receiveth it from the embodied Lamb, it is the elixir first of wisdom, then of the understanding of that wisdom, and finally it is the full-orbed enlightenment of the soul. And the water poured by the Guru into the upraised chalice of the chela shall be in him a well of water springing up into everlasting life. And the chela that believeth upon the Lamb, the embodied Guru, as the scripture hath said: out of his belly shall flow rivers of living water[102].

And so cometh Maitreya to initiate you in the initiation of water and in your individual God-mastery of the emotions – the energies of Alpha and Omega chaliced within the desire body and released through the ten-petaled chakra of the solar plexus, the *belly*. This mighty flow of rivers of living water is the veritable sign of the living chelas of the living Guru.

Let the desire body be cleared! Let the motive of the heart be purified! Let all of your desiring be the desiring of God within you to restore the soul to the balanced flow of water as the descending life-giving flow of Alpha and Omega! Lo, it is that sacred fire which is the rising caduceus held in the balance of the plus and the minus by your meditation upon the descending/ascending currents as water and fire commingling, life-giving! So let the water of life purify the soul! So let the sacred fire reinfuse the cells of the living body of God one by one with the personal presence of the Word! Behold the image of the Lord Christ and of his Lamb in every cell of the body of God, worlds without end!

You call me Sanat Kumara, and you know me as the one who stood before the cosmic council known as the Council of the One Hundred and Forty and Four. You know me because you were witnesses to my plea made for and on behalf of the evolutions of earth who no longer knew the presence of the Lamb, who by disobedience were cut off from the living Guru. You know me as the one who volunteered to embody the threefold flame within the earth unto the evolutions

---

[102] 1 John 4:14; 7:38.

evolving within the seven planes of being – fire, air, water, and earth.

The Cosmic Council had decreed the dissolution of earth and her evolutions because the souls of her children no longer worshiped the Trinity in the threefold flame of life[*] burning upon the altar of the heart. They had become the sheep gone astray. Their attention fixed upon the outer manifestation, they had willfully, ignorantly abandoned the inner walk with God. They knew not the hidden man of the heart,[103] that blessed Ishwara, and the seven candles no longer burned in the seven windows. Men and women had become hollow, their chakras black holes in time and space; and their vacated temples became the tombs of the dead; and the spirits of the dead took up their abode within their hollowed-out houses. Thus they received the judgment of the One Hundred and Forty and Four even as their descendants would hear the denunciation of the Son of God.[104]

Thus the light of the temples had gone out, and the purpose to which God had created man – to be the temple of the living God – was no longer being fulfilled. One and all were the living dead, a Matter vessel without an ensouling light, an empty shell. Nowhere on earth was there a mystery school – not a chela, not a Guru, no initiates of the path of initiation unto Christhood.

The hour of the judgment had come, and the one seated upon the throne in the center of the twelve times

---

[*] The flame of the Christ that is the spark of Life anchored in the secret chamber of the heart of the sons and daughters of God and the children of God. The sacred trinity of Power, Wisdom, and Love that is the manifestation of the sacred fire. (See "A Trilogy on the Threefold Flame of Life," in *Saint Germain On Alchemy*, pp. 265-352.)

[103] 1 Pet. 3:4.

[104] Matt. 23:27, 28.

twelve hierarchies of light had pronounced the word that was the unanimous consensus of all: Let earth and her evolutions be rolled up as a scroll and lit as a taper of the sacred fire. Let all energies misqualified be returned to the Great Central Sun for repolarization. Let energy misused be realigned and recharged with the light of Alpha and Omega, once again to be infused by the Creator within the ongoing creation of worlds without end.

The requirement of the law for the saving of Terra[*]? It was that one who should qualify as the embodied Guru, the Lamb, should be present in the physical octave to hold the balance and to keep the threefold flame of life for and on behalf of every living soul. It is the law of the One that the meditation of the one upon the Eternal Christos may count for the many until the many once again become accountable for their words and their works and can begin to bear the burden of their light as well as the karma of their relative good and evil.

I chose to be that one. I volunteered to be a flaming son of righteousness unto earth and her evolutions.

After considerable deliberation, the Cosmic Council and the Nameless One gave their approval of my petition, and the dispensation for a new divine plan for earth and her evolutions came into being. For cosmic law so states that when a hierarch of certain degrees and dimensions of cosmic consciousness volunteers to be the shepherd of lifewaves that are the lost sheep, the petition must be granted. Where there is no Guru, there can be no chelas; where there is no shepherd, there can be no sheep. As it is written: smite the shepherd, and the sheep are scattered.[105]

---

[*] Terra (Lat.) – Earth.
[105] Zech. 13:7.

But the Guru may be given opportunity to be Guru only for a certain cycle; and if at the end of that cycle the members of a lifewave by their recalcitrance and hardness of heart have not responded as chelas to the heart flame of the Guru, then the Guru must withdraw. And that which might have been may not be, and to no other hierarch then will the dispensation be given.

Thus I knelt before the great white throne of the Nameless One and he said unto me, "My son, Sanat Kumara, thou shalt sit upon the great white throne before the evolutions of earth. Thou shalt be to them the Lord God in the highest. Verily, thou shalt be the highest manifestation of the Deity which shall be given unto them until, through the path of initiation, their souls shall rise to thy throne of awareness and stand before thee in praise of the I AM THAT I AM which thou art. In that day when they shall rise up and say, 'Blessing and honour and glory and power be unto him that sitteth upon the throne and unto the Lamb for ever and ever' – behold, their redemption draweth nigh."

And he said unto me, "Thus unto the evolutions of earth thou shalt be Alpha and Omega, the beginning and the ending, saith the I AM THAT I AM, which is and which was and which is to come, the Almighty." And he placed upon me his mantle of sponsorship of the Father unto the Son which would become in me his sponsorship of a lifewave that he now made my own. It was a trust. It was the initiation of the Father in the Son.

And I knelt before the Nameless One and I worshiped God, saying, "Thou art worthy, O Lord, to receive glory and honour and power; for thou hast created all things, and for thy pleasure they are and were created."[106] And he, the Great Guru, repeated the

---

[106] Rev. 4:11.

approbation, thus completing the circle of devotion. He acknowledged the light that he and he alone had placed within my heart as the flaming image of himself, and to that image he said, "Thou art worthy, O Lord, to receive glory and honour and power: for thou hast created all things, and for thy pleasure they are and were created."

Thus I am in the Father and the Father is in me and we are one, worlds without end. And without that oneness, there can be no petition and no dispensation no matter what your level of evolution.

And the Council of the One Hundred and Forty and Four, forming a single solar ring around the great white throne, intoned the Word with the great beings of light, forming the inner circle round about the throne and saying, "Holy, holy, holy, Lord God Almighty, which was, and is, and is to come."[107] And I heard the echo of their chant of the "Holy, holy, holy" all the way home to the morning star, to my twin flame whom you know as Venus, and to the sons and daughters of the Love Star.

Winged messengers of light had announced my coming and the disposition of the Cosmic Council and the dispensation granted. The six – my brothers, the Holy Kumaras, who sustain with me the seven flames of the seven rays – Mighty Victory and his legions, our daughter Meta, and many servant sons and daughters whom you know today as the ascended masters welcomed me in a grand reception. That evening, the joy of opportunity was mingled with the sorrow that the sense of separation brings. I had chosen a voluntary exile upon a dark star. And though it was destined to be Freedom's Star, all knew it would be for me a long dark night of the soul.

---

[107] Rev. 4:8.

Then all at once from the valleys and the mountains there appeared a great gathering of my children. It was the souls of the hundred and forty and four thousand approaching our palace of light. They spiraled nearer and nearer as twelve companies singing the song of freedom, of love, and of victory. Their mighty chorusing echoed throughout elemental life, and angelic choirs hovered nigh. As we watched from the balcony, Venus and I, we saw the thirteenth company robed in white. It was the royal priesthood of the Order of the Melchizedek, the anointed ones who kept the flame and the law in the center of this hierarchical unit.

When all of their numbers had assembled, ring upon ring upon ring surrounding our home, and their hymn of praise and adoration to me was concluded, their spokesman stood before the balcony to address us on behalf of the great multitude. It was the soul of the one you know and love today as the Lord of the World, Gautama Buddha. And he addressed us, saying, "O Ancient of Days, we have heard of the covenant which God hath made with thee this day and of thy commitment to keep the flame of life until some among earth's evolutions should be quickened and once again renew their vow to be bearers of the flame. O Ancient of Days, thou art to us our Guru, our very life, our God. We will not leave thee comfortless. We will go with thee. We will not leave thee for one moment without the ring upon ring of our chelaship. We will come to earth. We will prepare the way. We will keep the flame in thy name."

And so as the Lord God directed me, I chose from among them four hundred servant sons and daughters who would precede the hundred and forty and four thousand to prepare for their coming. For though they knew the darkness of the darkest star, in reality they did not know, as I knew, the real meaning of the sacrifice which they now were offering to make in the name of their Guru.

We wept in joy, Venus and I and all of the hundred and forty and four thousand. And the tears that flowed on that memorable evening burned as the living sacred fire flowing as the water of life from the great white throne and the Cosmic Council, our sponsors.

I shall come again to continue with the history that unfolds from the folds of the garment of memory of the Ancient of Days.

O my children, I AM still your

Sanat Kumara

Let's return to the Third Root Race

As has become clear from the foregoing narration, man in his evolution goes through all the stages of development successively. Once upon a time we were minerals on earth, then plants, animals* and, finally, we became people. And, as people, we incarnate in each of the seven races**. Therefore, the information, given in *The Secret Doctrine* and rested on the unrevealed sources, available only for the Initiated and relating to the First, Second, Third and the following Races, should be considered as our history. It is precisely we who were embodied on the continent Lemuria millions years ago.

So, let's return to the Third Root Race. We stopped talking about that race at the moment when it was endowed with reason. At that time some of the Masters entered the bodies of people, others sent a spark and the third decided to wait for the Fourth Race to come.

Let's see how the last sub-races of the Third Root Race are described in *The Secret Doctrine*, what their religions, sciences, culture and the system of management were.

---

* We were minerals, plants and animals on globe **A**. See chapter "Conformity between the principles of man and Earth".
** The narration is simplified. Here we speak only about the fourth round on globe **D**.

"What was the religion of the Third and Fourth Races? In the common acceptation of the term, neither the Lemurians, nor yet their progeny, the Lemuro-Atlanteans, had any, as they knew no dogma, nor had they to believe on faith. No sooner had the mental eye of man been opened to understanding, than the Third Race felt itself one with the ever-present as the ever to be unknown and invisible ALL, the One Universal Deity. Endowed with divine powers, and feeling in himself his inner God, each felt he was a Man-God in his nature, though an animal in his physical Self. The struggle between the two began from the very day they tasted of the fruit of the Tree of Wisdom; a struggle for life between the spiritual and the psychic, the psychic and the physical. Those who conquered the lower principles by obtaining mastery over the body, joined the 'Sons of Light.' Those who fell victims to their lower natures, became the slaves of Matter. From 'Sons of Light and Wisdom' they ended by becoming the 'Sons of Darkness.' They had fallen in the battle of mortal life with Life immortal, and all those so fallen became the seed of the future generations of Atlanteans.[110]

"At the dawn of his consciousness, the man of the Third Root Race had thus no beliefs that could be called religion. That is to say, he was equally as ignorant of 'gay religions, full of pomp and gold' as of any system of faith or outward worship. But if the term is to be defined as the binding together of the masses in one form of reverence paid to those we feel higher than ourselves, of piety – as a feeling expressed

---

[110] The name is used here in the sense of, and as a synonym of "sorcerers". The Atlantean races were many, and lasted in their evolution for millions of years: all were not bad. They became so toward their end, as we (the fifth) are fast becoming now. (The footnote is copied from the book *The Secret Doctrine*)

by a child toward a loved parent – then even the earliest Lemurians had a religion – and a most beautiful one – from the very beginning of their intellectual life. Had they not their bright gods of the elements around them, and even within themselves?[111] Was not their childhood passed with, nursed and tendered by those who had given them life and called them forth to intelligent, conscious life? We are assured it was so, and we believe it. For the evolution of Spirit into matter could never have been achieved; nor would it have received its first impulse, had not the bright Spirits sacrificed their own respective super-ethereal essences to animate the man of clay, by endowing each of his inner principles with a portion, or rather, a reflection of that essence."[112]

"Their Science was innate in them. The Lemuro-Atlantean had no need of discovering and fixing in his memory that which his informing PRINCIPLE knew at the moment of its incarnation. Time alone, and the ever-growing obtuseness of the matter in which the Principles had clothed themselves, could, the one, weaken the memory of their pre-natal knowledge, the other, blunt and even extinguish every spark of the spiritual and divine in them."[113]

Lemurians were ruled by The Divine Rulers. This did not give a chance for the Evil connected with the misuse of the authority to manifest itself.

"That evil, Plato seems to see in the sameness or consubstantiality of the natures of the rulers and the

---

[111] The "Gods of the Elements" are by no means the Elementals. The latter are at best used by them as vehicles and materials in which to clothe themselves… (The footnote is copied from the book *The Secret Doctrine*)

[112] The Secret Doctrine, Vol. 2, p. 272.

[113] *Ibid.*, p. 285.

ruled, for he says that long before man built his cities, in the golden age, there was naught but happiness on earth, for there were no needs. Why? Because Saturn, knowing that man could not rule man, without injustice filling forthwith the universe through his whims and vanity, would not allow any mortal to obtain power over his fellow creatures. To do this the god used the same means we use ourselves with regard to our flocks. We do not place a bullock or a ram over our bullocks and rams, but give them a leader, a shepherd, i.e., a being of a species quite different from their own and of a superior nature. It is just what Saturn did. He loved mankind and placed to rule over it no mortal King or prince but – 'Spirits and genii daimoneß of a divine nature more excellent than that of man.' It was god, the Logos (the synthesis of the Host) who thus presiding over the genii, became the first shepherd and leader of men.[114] *When the world had ceased to be so governed and the gods retired, 'ferocious beasts devoured a portion of mankind.' 'Left to their own resources and industry, inventors then appeared among them successively and discovered fire, wheat, wine; and public gratitude deified them...' (Plato 'De Legibus' 1, iv.; in Crit. and in Politic)."*[115]

"As the Commentaries say:

Fruits and grain, unknown to Earth to that day, were brought by the 'Lords of Wisdom' for the benefit of those they ruled – from other lokas (spheres)..."[116]

---

[114] The Secret Doctrine explains and expounds that which Plato says, for it teaches that those "inventors" were gods and demi-gods (Devas and Rishis) who had become – some deliberately, some forced to by Karma – incarnated in man.

[115] The Secret Doctrine, Vol. 2, p. 373

[116] *Ibid.*, p. 373

The Lemurians *"...under the guidance of their divine Rulers, built large cities, cultivated arts and sciences, and knew astronomy, architecture and mathematics to perfection. This primeval civilization did not, as one may think, immediately follow their physiological transformation. Between the final evolution and the first city built, many hundred thousands of years had passed. Yet, we find the Lemurians in their sixth sub-race building their first rock-cities out of stone and lava. One of such great cities of primitive structure was built entirely of lava, some thirty miles west from where Easter Island now stretches its narrow piece of sterile ground, and was entirely destroyed by a series of volcanic eruptions. The oldest remains of Cyclopean buildings were all the handiwork of the Lemurians of the last sub-races..."*

"The first large cities, however, appeared on that region of the continent which is now known as the island of Madagascar. There were civilized people and savages in those days as there are now. Evolution achieved its work of perfection with the former, and Karma – its work of destruction on the latter. The Australians[117] and their like are the descendants of those, who, instead of vivifying the spark dropped into them by the 'Flames,' extinguished it by long generations of bestiality.[118] The Aryan nations could

---

[117] They belong to the last survivors of the seventh sub-race of the Third Race.

[118] See Stanza II. This would account for the great difference and variation between the intellectual capacities of races, nations, and individual men. While incarnating, and in other cases only informing the human vehicles evolved by the first brainless (manasless) race, the incarnating Powers and Principles had to make their choice between, and take into account, the past Karmas of the Monads, between which and their bodies they had to become the connecting link. Besides which, as correctly stated in "Esoteric Buddhism" (p. 30), "the fifth principle, or human (intellectual)

trace their descent through the Atlanteans from the more spiritual races of the Lemurians, in whom the 'Sons of Wisdom' had personally incarnated.

"It is with the advent of the divine Dynasties that the first civilizations were started. And while, in some regions of the Earth, a portion of mankind preferred leading a nomadic and patriarchal life, and in others savage man was hardly learning to build a fire and to protect himself against the Elements, his brothers – more favoured than he by their Karma, and helped by the divine intelligence which informed them – built cities, and cultivated arts and sciences. Nevertheless, and civilization notwithstanding, while their pastoral brethren enjoyed wondrous powers as their birthright, they, the builders, could now obtain theirs only gradually; even these being generally used for power over physical nature and selfish and unholy purposes. Civilization has ever developed the physical and the intellectual at the cost of the psychic and spiritual. The command and the guidance over his own psychic nature, which foolish men now associate with the supernatural, were with early Humanity innate and congenital, and came to man as naturally as walking and thinking."[119]

"It was the 'Golden Age' in those days of old, the age when the 'gods walked the earth, and mixed freely with the mortals.' Since then, the gods departed (i.e., became invisible), and later generations ended by worshipping their kingdoms – the Elements."[120]

The fall began from the first characteristic feature of each physical human – pride: "We are kings, we are

---

soul, in the majority of mankind is not even yet fully developed." (The footnote is copied from the book *The Secret Doctrine*)

[119] The Secret Doctrine, Vol. 2, p. 318-319

[120] *Ibid.*, p. 273

Gods!" All this started from the cult of the human body and ended in the cult of the related sexes.

"As the 'coats of skin' of men thickened, and they fell more and more into physical sin, the intercourse between physical and ethereal divine man was stopped. The veil of matter between the two planes became too dense for even the inner man to penetrate. The mysteries of Heaven and Earth, revealed to the Third Race by their celestial teachers in the days of their purity, became a great focus of light, the rays from which became necessarily weakened as they were diffused and shed upon an uncongenial, because too material soil. With the masses they degenerated into Sorcery, taking later on the shape of exoteric religions, of idolatry full of superstitions, and man-, or hero-worship. Alone a handful of primitive men – in whom the spark of divine Wisdom burnt bright, and only strengthened in its intensity as it got dimmer and dimmer with every age in those who turned it to bad purposes – remained the elect custodians of the

Mysteries revealed to mankind by the divine Teachers."[121]

"Gradually, mankind went down in stature, for, even before the real advent of the Fourth or Atlantean race, the majority of mankind had fallen into iniquity and sin, save the hierarchy of the 'Elect,' the followers and disciples of the 'Sons of Will and Yoga' – called later the 'Sons of the Fire Mist.'"[122]

---

[121] The Secret Doctrine, Vol. 2, p. 281
[122] *Ibid.*, p. 319

Lemuria

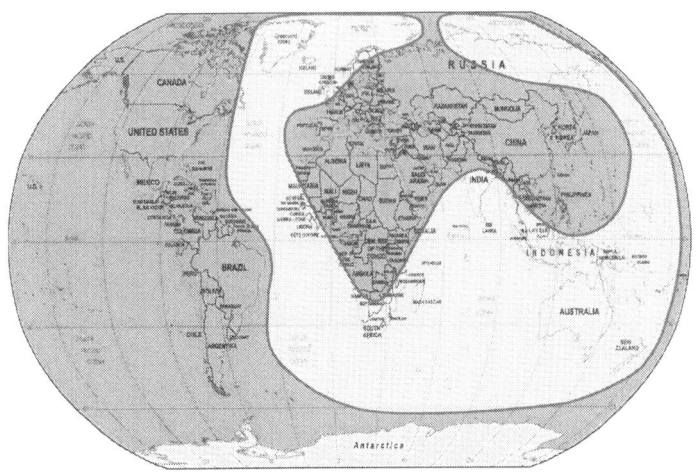

T he Third Root Race inhabited a vast U-shaped continent called in *The Secret Doctrine,* Lemuria. I tried to depict this continent in accordance with the description given in *The Secret Doctrine.* Certainly, it is only a broad-brush representation. The coastline, for sure, was more indented by peninsulas, cusps, creeks. A lot of isles were adjacent to the continent. Neither Europe, nor Africa, nor both Americas existed at that time, nor did the greater part of Asia.

I will give quotations from *The Secret Doctrine,* on the basis of which I have plotted my map.

"The great lost continent might have, perhaps, been situated south of Asia, extending from India to Tasmania"[123]

---

[123] The Secret Doctrine, Vol. 2, p. 221

"...the fragments of which must be sought in Madagascar, Ceylon, Sumatra, Java, Borneo, and the principal isle of Polynesia."[124]

"The high plateaux of Hindustan and Asia, according to this hypothesis, would only have been represented in those distant epochs by great islands contiguous to the central continent..."

"Apart from this fact, the supposition of an ancient continent in those latitudes, the vestiges of which may be found in the volcanic islands and mountainous surface of the Azores, the Canaries and Cape de Verdes, is not devoid of geographical probability."

"Moreover, when we cast a look on a planisphere, at the sight of the islands and islets strewn from the Malayan Archipelago to Polynesia, from the straits of Sunda to Easter Island, it is impossible, upon the hypothesis of continents preceding those which we inhabit, not to place there the most important of all."[125]

" 'Lemuria', as we have called the continent of the Third Race, was then a gigantic land[126]. It covered the whole area of space from the foot of the Himalayas, which separated it from the inland sea rolling its waves over what is now Tibet, Mongolia, and the great desert of Schamo (Gobi); from Chittagong, westward to Hardwar, and eastward to Assam. From thence, it stretched South across what is known to us as Southern India, Ceylon, and Sumatra; then embracing on its way, as we go South, Madagascar on

---

[124] *Ibid.*, p. 222

[125] *Ibid.*, p. 222-223

[126] As shown in the Introduction, it stands to reason that neither the name of Lemuria nor even Atlantis are the real archaic names of the lost continents, but have been adopted by us for the sake of clearness... (The footnote is copied from the book *The Secret Doctrine*)

its right hand and Australia and Tasmania on its left, it ran down to within a few degrees of the Antarctic Circle; when, from Australia, an inland region on the Mother Continent in those ages, it extended far into the Pacific Ocean, not only beyond Rapa-nui (Teapy, or Easter Island) which now lies in latitude 26 S., and longitude 110 W."[127]

"Easter Isle, for instance, belongs to the earliest civilisation of the Third Race. Submerged with the rest, a volcanic and sudden uplifting of the Ocean floor, raised the small relic of the Archaic ages untouched, with its volcano and statues, during the Champlain epoch of northern polar submersion, as a standing witness to the existence of Lemuria."[128]

"But here an explanation is needed. No confusion need arise as regards the postulation of a Northern 'Lemuria.' The prolongation of that great continent into the North Atlantic Ocean is in no way subversive of the opinions so widely held as to the site of the lost

---

[127] The Secret Doctrine, Vol. 2, p. 323
[128] *Ibid.*, p. 327

Atlantis, and one corroborates the other. It must be noted that the Lemuria, which served as the cradle of the Third Root-Race, not only embraced a vast area in the Pacific and Indian Oceans, but extended in the shape of a horse-shoe past Madagascar, round 'South Africa' (then a mere fragment in process of formation), through the Atlantic up to Norway."[129]

"...Sweden and Norway had formed part and parcel of ancient Lemuria, and also of Atlantis on the European side, just as Eastern and Western Siberia and Kamschatka had belonged to it, on the Asiatic."[130]

It should be said that the part of the continent Lemuria which was situated on the place of the Atlantic ocean and became in the future a new continent – Atlantis – was raised from the ocean bottom much later than the basic part of the continent.

Lemuro-Atlantes who inhibited this part of Lemuria became the new Fourth Root Race afterwards.

In accordance with the Great Cosmic Law for each race a new continent is brought into being. On this continent the race grows, develops, gets old and the remainder of this race sink to the ocean bottom together with the continent in due time. But nature is already preparing a new continent for a new race by that time.

"For the Secret Doctrine teaches that, during this Round, there must be seven terrestrial pralayas, three occasioned by the change in the inclination of the earth's axis. It is a law which acts at its appointed time, and not at all blindly, as science may think, but in strict accordance and harmony with Karmic law. In

---

[129] *Ibid.*, p. 333
[130] *Ibid.*, p. 402

Occultism this inexorable law is referred to as 'the great ADJUSTER.' "[131]

"Thus, since... Humanity appeared on this Earth, there have already been four such axial disturbances; when the old continents – save the first one – were sucked in by the oceans, other lands appeared, and huge mountain chains arose where there had been none before. The face of the Globe was completely changed each time; the survival of the fittest nations and races was secured through timely help; and the unfit ones – the failures – were disposed of by being swept off the earth. Such sorting and shifting does not happen between sunset and sunrise, as one may think, but requires several thousands of years before the new house is set in order." [132]

The time came, and the vast continent Lemuria started to break down into smaller continents.

"Lemuria was not submerged as Atlantis was, but was sunk under the waves, owing to earthquakes and subterranean fires, as Great Britain and Europe will be one day." [133]

"According to the explanation in the Commentary, to a decrease of velocity in the earth's rotation:

'When the Wheel runs at the usual rate, its extremities (the poles) agree with its middle circle (equator), when it runs slower and tilts in every direction, there is a great disturbance on the face of the Earth. The waters flow toward the two ends, and new lands arise in the middle belt (equatorial

---

[131] The Secret Doctrine, Vol. 2, p. 329

[132] *Ibid.*, p. 330

[133] *Ibid.*, p. 266

lands), while those at the ends are subject to pralayas by submersion...'
And again:

'Thus the wheel (the Earth) is subject to, and regulated by, the Spirit of the Moon, for the breath of its waters (tides). Toward the close of the age (Kalpa) of a great (root) race, the regents of the moon (the Pitar fathers, or Pitris) begin drawing harder, and thus flatten the wheel about its belt, when it goes down in some places and swells in others, and the swelling running toward the extremities (poles) new lands will arise and old ones be sucked in. '"[134]

Gradually only separate islands remained after the gigantic continent, and they quickly disappeared one after another on the ocean bottom.

"Lemuria is said[135] to have perished about 700,000 years before the commencement of what is now called the Tertiary age (the Eocene[136]). "[137]

---

[134] *Ibid.*, p. 324

[135] "Esoteric Buddhism," p. 55. (The footnote is copied from the book *The Secret Doctrine*)

[136] In the "Great Soviet Encyclopedia" the tertiary period is subdivided into two: the Palaeogene and the Neogene. The Neogene period started about 25 million years ago. The Palaeogene period lasted from 68 million years ago to 25 million years ago. The Eocene period is given as the middle part of the Palaeogene period. A simple arithmetic calculation provides the date when the continent Lemuria ceased to exist. This happened over 50 million years ago. However, physical humanity, according to the data of *The Secret Doctrine*, started to exist only about 18 million years ago. I cannot explain this discrepancy. It is probably that the time when the continent ceased to exist is concealed on purpose. Yet many things in *The Secret Doctrine* are given in vague terms and with the explicit purpose to confuse the profane investigator. However, modern science in various geological schools attributes to the geological periods completely different durations.

[137] The Secret Doctrine, Vol. 2, p. 313

The largest part which remained from the continent of Lemuria is Australia. This continent has suffered fewer changes than any other continent – with regard to its flora and fauna. *The Secret Doctrine* explains this in such a way:

"Where is the raison d'etre for such a 'curse of retardation'? It is simply because the nature of the environment develops pari passu with the race concerned. Correspondences rule in every quarter. The survivors of those later Lemurians, who escaped the destruction of their fellows when the main continent was submerged, became the ancestors of a portion of the present native tribes. Being a very low sub-race... their stock has since existed in an environment strongly subjected to the law of retardation. Australia is one of the oldest lands now above the waters, and in the senile decrepitude of old age, its 'virgin soil' notwithstanding. It can produce no new forms, unless helped by new and fresh races, and artificial cultivation and breeding."[138]

This is a rather significant fact and commentary. This proves that only man by means of changing his consciousness is able to change this world.

---

[138] The Secret Doctrine, Vol. 2, p. 197

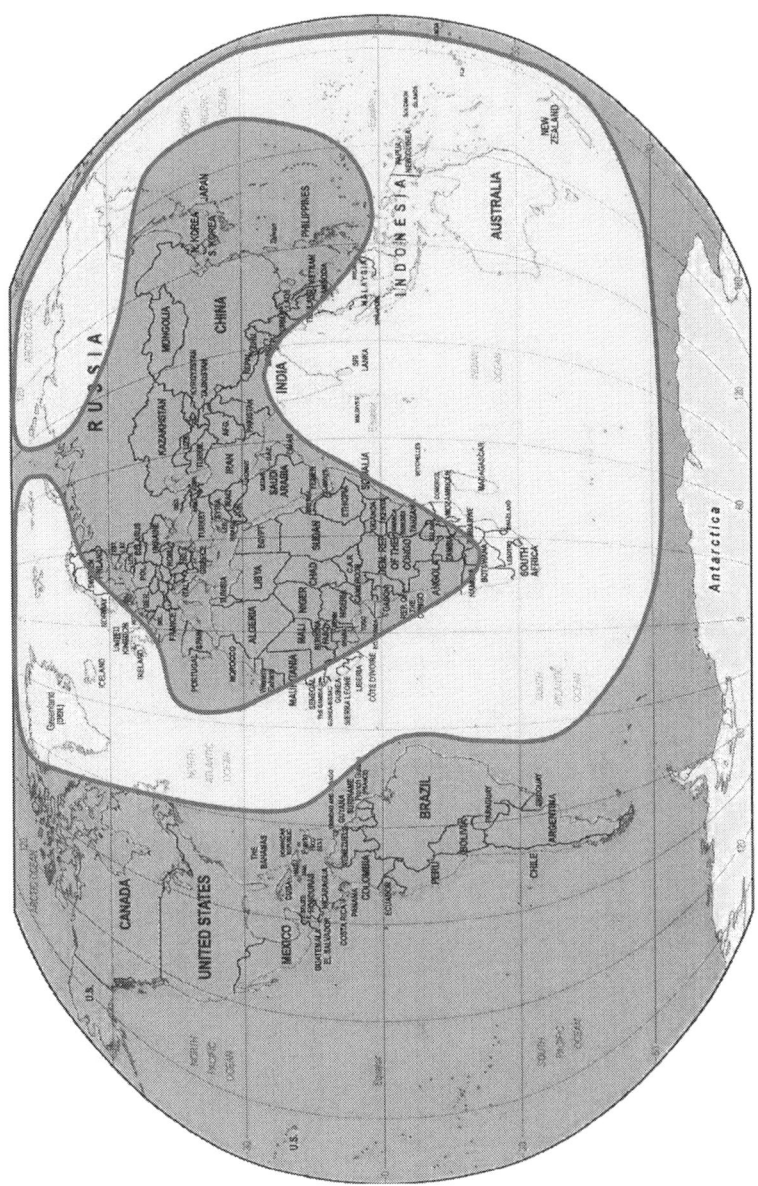

The map of Lemuria, restored by the author according to the description given in *The Secret Doctrine* by H.P. Blavatsky

The Fourth Root Race.
Atlantis

Let's have a look now at what *The Secret Doctrine* tells us about the Fourth Root Race, in other words the Race of Atlantes.

"The Atlantic portion of Lemuria was the geological basis of what is generally known as Atlantis. The latter, indeed, must be regarded rather as a development of the Atlantic prolongation of Lemuria, than as an entirely new mass of land upheaved to meet the special requirements of the Fourth Root-Race. Just as in the case of Race-evolution, so in that of the shifting and re-shifting of continental masses, no hard and fast line can be drawn where a new order ends and another begins. Continuity in natural processes is never broken. Thus the Fourth Race Atlanteans were developed from a nucleus of Northern Lemurian Third Race Men, centred, roughly speaking, toward a point of land in what is now the mid-Atlantic Ocean. Their continent was formed by the coalescence of many islands and peninsulas which were upheaved in the ordinary course of time and became ultimately the true home of the great Race known as the Atlanteans. After this consummation was once attained it follows, as stated on the highest 'occult' authority, that

> *'Lemuria should no more be confounded with the Atlantis Continent, than Europe with America.'('Esoteric Buddhism', p. 58.)"*[139]

---

[139] The Secret Doctrine, Vol. 2, p. 333-334

The Atlanteans *"were born with a sight, which embraced all living things... whose sight was unlimited, and who knew all things at once."*[140]

From the very start the Race of Atlantes split into two different races, which were *"distinct physically and especially morally; both deeply versed in primeval wisdom and the secrets of nature; mutually antagonistic in their struggle, during the course and progress of their double evolution."*[141]

These were the Adepts of the left hand, magi and wizards, who used their inborn abilities to satisfy their own aims, and the Adepts of the right hand who had always formed the mainstay of all the Schools of Initiations that had ever existed on earth.

"Thus the first Atlantean races, born on the Lemurian Continent, separated from their earliest tribes into the righteous and the unrighteous; into those who worshipped the one unseen Spirit of Nature, the ray of which man feels within himself – or the Pantheists, and those who offered fanatical worship to the Spirits of the Earth, the dark Cosmic, anthropomorphic Powers, with whom they made alliance."[142]

These latter laid the ground for the future exoteric external religions based on cult, rituals and dogmas.

Atlantes considerably exceeded our present humanity in stature. Many people's legends that have survived to the present day include the mention of giants. Even in the Russian folk tales there are epic heroes, the bogatyrs. These mighty people of great

---

[140] *Ibid.*, p. 221
[141] *Ibid.*, p. 372
[142] *Ibid.*, p. 273

glory were called Kabirs among the Egyptians and Phoenicians, Titans among the Greeks, Rakshases and Daityas among the Hindu peoples.

In the times of the Atlantes the Divine dynasties were ruling – the incarnations of the higher spirits. But since those were physical incarnations, duality was inherent in these kings. Their divine nature was tinged with imperfections characteristic of people. Let us remember what *The Secret Doctrine* says about it: ***"Once landed on, and having touched this planet of dense matter, no snow-white wings of the highest angel can remain immaculate, or the Avatar (or incarnation) be perfect, as every such Avatar is the fall of a God into generation."***[143]

"…they were the Lemuro-Atlanteans, the first who had a dynasty of Spirit-Kings, not of Manes, or 'ghosts,' as some believe, but of actual living Devas (or demi-gods or Angels, again) who had assumed bodies to rule over them, and who, in their turn, instructed them in arts and sciences. Only, as they were rupa or material Spirits, these Dhyanis were not always good. Their King Thevetata was one of the latter, and it is under the evil influence of this King-Demon that… the Atlantis-race became a nation of wicked magicians."

"In consequence of this, war was declared, the story of which would be too long to narrate…"[144]

Apart from the sin of abusing their Divine gifts, the Atlantes also committed a pretty earthly sin.

"The Esoteric doctrine… accuses them of having committed the (to us) abominable crime of breeding

---

[143] The Secret Doctrine, Vol. 2, p. 483
[144] *Ibid.*, p. 222

with so-called 'animals,' and thus producing a truly pithecoid species, now extinct.

"A careful perusal of the Commentaries would make one think that the Being that the new 'incarnate' bred with, was called an 'animal,' not because he was no human being, but rather because he was so dissimilar physically and mentally to the more perfect races, which had developed physiologically at an earlier period. Remember Stanza VII. and what is said in its first verse (24th):– that when the 'Sons of Wisdom' came to incarnate the first time, some of them incarnated fully, others projected into the forms only a spark, while some of the shadows were left over from being filled and perfected, till the Fourth Race. Those races, then, which 'remained destitute of knowledge,' or those again which were left 'mindless,' remained as they were, even after the natural separation of the sexes. It is these who committed the first cross-breeding, so to speak, and bred monsters; and it is from the descendants of these that the Atlanteans chose their wives."[145]

"Hence the assertion that many of us are now working off the effects of the evil Karmic causes produced by us in Atlantean bodies. The Law of KARMA is inextricably interwoven with that of Re-incarnation.

"It is only the knowledge of the constant re-births of one and the same individuality throughout the life-cycle; the assurance that the same MONADS – among whom are many Dhyan-Chohans, or the 'Gods' themselves – have to pass through the 'Circle of Necessity,' rewarded or punished by such rebirth for

[145] *Ibid.,* p. 286

the suffering endured or crimes committed in the former life; that those very Monads, which entered the empty, senseless shells, or astral figures of the First Race emanated by the Pitris, are the same who are now amongst us – nay, ourselves, perchance; it is only this doctrine, we say, that can explain to us the mysterious problem of Good and Evil, and reconcile man to the terrible and apparent injustice of life. Nothing but such certainty can quiet our revolted sense of justice. For, when one unacquainted with the noble doctrine looks around him, and observes the inequalities of birth and fortune, of intellect and capacities; when one sees honour paid fools and profligates, on whom fortune has heaped her favours by mere privilege of birth, and their nearest neighbour, with all his intellect and noble virtues – far more deserving in every way – perishing of want and for lack of sympathy; when one sees all this and has to turn away, helpless to relieve the undeserved suffering, one's ears ringing and heart aching with the cries of pain around him – that blessed knowledge of Karma alone prevents him from cursing life and men, as well as their supposed Creator."[146]

The time came, "the edges of earth opened" and the Atlantean continent submerged under the water at a fast clip. This took place between 850 000 and 700 000 years ago.

I will give in full a rather long passage from *The Secret Doctrine* where this event is described in detail. *The Secret Doctrine* concurrently hypothesises, or more likely asserts, that the flight of the Israelites from Egypt, described in the Book of Exodus in the Bible, represents not the original historical event, but merely a

---

[146] The Secret Doctrine, Vol. 2, p. 303

paraphrase of the events connected with the submergence of Atlantis and drawn from a more ancient source.

"Several times the writer has put to herself the question: 'Is the story of Exodus – in its details at least – as narrated in the Old Testament, original? Or is it, like the story of Moses himself and many others, simply another version of the legends told of the Atlanteans?' For who, upon hearing the story told of the latter, will fail to perceive the great similarity of the fundamental features? The anger of 'God' at the obduracy of Pharaoh, his command to the 'chosen' ones, to spoil the Egyptians, before departing, of their 'jewels of silver and jewels of gold'[147]; and finally the Egyptians and their Pharaoh drowned in the Red Sea. For here is a fragment of the earlier story from the Commentary:–

"And the 'great King of the dazzling Face', the chief of all the Yellow-faced, was sad, seeing the sins of the Black-faced.

"He sent his air-vehicles (Viwan) to all his brother-chiefs (chiefs of other nations and tribes) with pious men within, saying:

'Prepare. Arise ye men of the good law, and cross the land while (yet) dry.'

'The Lords of the storm are approaching. Their chariots are nearing the land. One night and two days only shall the Lords of the Dark Face (the Sorcerers) live on this patient land. She is doomed, and they have to descend with her. The nether Lords of the Fires (the Gnomes and fire Elementals) are preparing their magic Agneyâstra (fire-weapons

---

[147] Exod. xi. (The footnote is copied from the book *The Secret Doctrine*)

worked by magic). But the Lords of the Dark Eye ('Evil Eye') are stronger than they (the Elementals) and they are the slaves of the mighty ones. They are versed in Ashtar (Vidya, the highest magical knowledge). Come and use yours (i.e., your magic powers, in order to counteract those of the Sorcerers). Let every lord of the Dazzling Face (an adept of the White Magic) cause the Viwan of every lord of the Dark Face to come into his hands (or possession), lest any (of the Sorcerers) should by its means escape from the waters, avoid the rod of the Four, (Karmic deities) and save his wicked (followers, or people)'.

'May every yellow face send sleep from himself (mesmerize?) to every black face. May even they (the Sorcerers) avoid pain and suffering. May every man true to the Solar Gods bind (paralyze) every man under the lunar gods, lest he should suffer or escape his destiny.

'And may every yellow face offer of his life-water (blood) to the speaking animal[148] of a black face, lest he awaken his master.

'The hour has struck, the black night is ready...'

. . . .

'Let their destiny be accomplished. We are the servants of the great Four[149]. May the Kings of light return.'

---

[148] Some wonderful, artificially-made beast, similar in some way to Frankenstein's creation, which spoke and warned his master of every approaching danger. The master was a "black magician", the mechanical animal was informed by a djin, an Elemental, according to the accounts. The blood of a pure man alone could destroy him. *Vide* Part II., xxvii., "Seven in Astronomy, Science, and Magic". (The footnote is copied from the book *The Secret Doctrine*)

[149] The four Karmic gods, called the Four Maharajahs in the Stanzas (see *The Secret Doctrine*).

"The great King fell upon his dazzling Face and wept...

"When the Kings assembled the waters had already moved. . . .

"(But) the nations had now crossed the dry lands. They were beyond the water mark. Their Kings reached them in their Viwans, and led them on to the lands of Fire and Metal (East and North)."

"Still, in another passage, it is said:–

"Stars (meteors) showered on the lands of the black Faces; but they slept.

"The speaking beasts (the magic watchers) kept quiet.

"The nether lords waited for orders, but they came not, for their masters slept.

"The waters arose, and covered the valleys from one end of the Earth to the other. High lands remained, the bottom of the Earth (the lands of the antipodes) remained dry. There dwelt those who escaped; the men of the yellow-faces and of the straight eye (the frank and sincere people).

"When the Lords of the Dark Faces awoke and bethought themselves of their Viwans in order to escape from the rising waters, they found them gone."

"Then a passage shows some of the more powerful magicians of the 'Dark Face' – who awoke earlier than the others pursuing those who had 'spoilt them' and who were in the rear-guard, for – 'the nations that were led away, were as thick as the stars of the milky way,' says a more modern Commentary, written in Sanskrit only.

"Like as a dragon-snake uncoils slowly its body, so the Sons of men, led on by the Sons of Wisdom,

99

opened their folds, and spreading out, expanded like a running stream of sweet waters... many of the faint-hearted among them perished on their way. But most were saved."

"Yet the pursuers, 'whose heads and chests soared high above the water,' chased them 'for three lunar terms' until finally reached by the rising waves, they perished to the last man, the soil sinking under their feet and the earth engulfing those who had desecrated her.

"This sounds a good deal like the original material upon which the similar story in Exodus was built many hundred thousands of years later. The biography of Moses, the story of his birth, childhood and rescue from the Nile by Pharaoh's daughter, is now shown to have been adapted from the Chaldean narrative about Sargon. And if so, the Assyrian tile in the British Museum being a good proof of it, why not that of the Jews robbing the Egyptians of their jewels, the death of Pharaoh and his army, and so on? The gigantic magicians of Ruta and Daitya, the 'lords of the Dark Face', may have become in the later narrative the Egyptian Magi, and the yellow-faced nations of the Fifth Race, the virtuous sons of Jacob, the 'chosen people'."[150]

A small island remained after the continent of Atlantis, described by Plato and called by him Poseidonis. In its turn, it submerged under the water about 10 thousand years ago.

"The secret teachings show that the 'Deluge' overtook the Fourth, giant Race, not on account of their depravity, or because they had become 'black

---

[150] The Secret Doctrine, Vol. 2, p. 426-429

with sin,' but simply because such is the fate of every continent, which like everything else under our Sun – is born, lives, becomes decrepit, and dies. This was when the Fifth Race was in its infancy. [151]

"Thus the giants perished – the magicians and the sorcerers, adds the fancy of popular tradition, but 'all holy saved,' and alone the 'unholy were destroyed.' This was due, however, as much to the prevision of the 'holy' ones, who had not lost the use of their 'third eye,' as to Karma and natural law. Speaking of the subsequent race (our Fifth Humanity), the commentary says:

> *"Alone the handful of those Elect, whose divine instructors had gone to inhabit that Sacred Island – 'from whence the last Saviour will come' – now kept mankind from becoming one-half the exterminator of the other [as mankind does now – H.P.B.]. It (mankind) became divided. Two-thirds of it were ruled by Dynasties of lower, material Spirits of the earth, who took possession of the easily accessible bodies; one-third remained faithful, and joined with the nascent Fifth Race – the divine Incarnates. When the Poles moved (for the fourth time) this did not affect those who were protected, and who had separated from the Fourth Race. Like the Lemurians – alone the ungodly Atlanteans perished, and 'were seen no more'...* "[152]

The Instructors of mankind, the hierarchy of the higher entities *"have found refuge in the great desert*

---

[151] Two hundred thousand years before the submersion of the main continent of the Atlantis the representatives of the new – Fifth Root Race – the Arians – started to appear amidst the race of Atlanteans.
[152] The Secret Doctrine, Vol. 2, p. 350

of Gobi, where they still reside invisible to all, and defended from approach by hosts of Spirits."[153]

And yet, what does *The Secret Doctrine* say about whether any representatives of the Fourth Root Race have remained on earth thus far? Indeed, yes.

"The majority of mankind belongs to the seventh sub-race of the Fourth Root-Race – the above-mentioned Chinamen and their off-shoots and branchlets. (Malayans, Mongolians, Tibetans, Hungarians, Finns, and even the Esquimaux are all remnants of this last offshoot.)"[154]

"...there is in the Malay race (a sub-race of the Fourth Root Race) a singular diversity of stature; the members of the Polynesian family (Tahitians, Samoans, and Tonga islanders) are of a higher stature than the rest of mankind; but the Indian tribes and the inhabitants of the Indo-Chinese countries are decidedly below the general average. This is easily explained. The Polynesians belong to the very earliest of the surviving sub-races, the others to the very last and transitory stock. As the Tasmanians are now completely extinct, and the Australians rapidly dying out, so will the other old races soon follow."[155]

One more interesting fact is referred to in *The Secret Doctrine*. The first pyramids of Egypt were constructed by the Atlantes long before the advent of an Egyptian tribe from the east (the number 78 000 years ago can be considered as the tentative time of the construction of the pyramids). The Egyptians and the

---

[153] The Secret Doctrine, Vol. 2, p. 372
[154] *Ibid.*, p. 178
[155] *Ibid.*, p. 332

Aryan Indians represent kindred ethnic groups of the Fifth Race.

The Fifth Root Race

FOURTH

J ust exactly as the ~~Third~~ Race was gradually forming within the ~~Fourth~~ Race, the Fifth Race in its turn started to form within the Race of Atlantes. This happened about 200 thousand years before the submergence of the main continent of Atlantis or about one million years ago.

At present the fifth sub-race of the Fifth Root Race is incarnated and the sixth sub-race starts to incarnate.

In order to clarify the situation with the sub-races it is necessary to take into consideration the following:

1. In each Manvantara the monads incarnate in every one of the seven races, passing in their development through seven Rounds. *"...this one is the Fourth, and we are in the Fifth Root-Race, at present.*

2. Each Root-Race has seven sub-races.

3. Each sub-race has, in its turn, seven ramifications, which may be called Branch or 'Family' races.

4. The little tribes, shoots, and offshoots of the last-named are countless and depend on Karmic action.

"Examine the 'genealogical tree' hereto appended, and you will understand. The illustration is purely diagrammatic, and is only intended to assist the reader in obtaining a slight grasp of the subject, amidst the confusion which exists between the terms which have been used at different times for the divisions of Humanity. It is also here attempted to express in figures – but only within approximate limits, for the sake of comparison – the duration of time through which it is possible to definitely distinguish one division from another. It would only lead to hopeless confusion if any attempt were made to give accurate

dates to a few; for the Races, Sub-Races, etc., etc., down to their smallest ramifications, overlap and are entangled with each other until it is nearly impossible to separate them.

GENEALOGICAL TREE OF THE FIFTH ROOT RACE

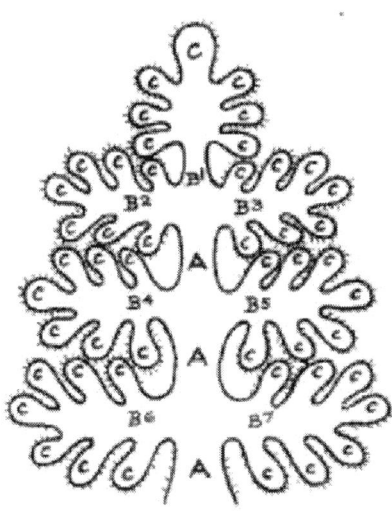

"*The human Race has been compared to a tree, and this serves admirably as an illustration.*

"*The main stem of a tree may be compared to the* **ROOT-RACE (A).**

"*Its larger limbs to the various* **SUB-RACES;** *seven in number (B^1, B^2, B^3 etc).*

"*On each of these limbs are seven* **BRANCHES, OR FAMILY-RACES. (C).**

"*After this the cactus-plant is a better illustration, for its fleshy 'leaves' are covered with sharp spines, each of which may be compared to a nation or tribe of human beings.*

"*Now our Fifth Root-Race has already been in existence – as a race sui generis and quite free from its parent stem about 1,000,000 years; therefore it must be inferred that each of the four preceding Sub-Races has lived approximately 210,000 years; thus each Family-Race has an average existence of about 30,000 years. Thus the European 'Family Race' has still a good many thousand years to run, although the nations or the innumerable spines upon it, vary with each succeeding 'season' of three or four thousand years. It is somewhat curious to mark the comparative approximation of duration between the lives of a 'Family-Race' and a 'Sidereal year.'*

"The knowledge of the foregoing, and the accurately correct division, formed part and parcel of the Mysteries, where these Sciences were taught to the disciples, and where they were transmitted by one hierophant to another."[156]

Exactly as in the times of the Third and the Fourth Races the Heavenly Instructors did not leave the Fifth Race without care and nurturance. For example, it is known that *"after having abandoned the Atlanteans to their doom, returned (or redescended, rather) during the third Sub-Race of the Fifth, in order to reveal to saved humanity the mysteries of their birth-place – the sidereal Heavens."*[157]

"The duration of the periods that separate, in space and time, the Fourth from the Fifth Race – in the historical or even the legendary beginnings of the latter – is too tremendous for us to offer, even to a Theosophist, any more detailed accounts of them. During the course of the post-diluvian ages – marked at certain periodical epochs by the most terrible cataclysms – too many races and nations were born, and have disappeared almost without leaving a trace,

---

[156] The Secret Doctrine, Vol. 2, p. 434-435
[157] *Ibid.*, p. 436

for any one to offer any description of the slightest value concerning them. Whether the Masters of Wisdom have a consecutive and full history of our race from its incipient stage down to the present times; whether they possess the uninterrupted record of man since he became the complete physical being, and became thereby the king of the animals and master on this earth – is not for the writer to say. Most probably they have, and such is our own personal conviction. But if so, this knowledge is only for the highest Initiates, who do not take their students into their confidence. The writer can, therefore, give but what she has herself been taught, and no more. But even this will appear to the profane reader rather as a weird, fantastic dream, than as a possible reality.

"This is only natural and as it should be, since for years such was the impression made upon the humble writer of these pages herself. Born and bred in European, matter-of-fact and presumably civilized countries, she assimilated the foregoing with the utmost difficulty. But there are proofs of a certain character which become irrefutable and are undeniable in the long run, to every earnest and unprejudiced mind. For a series of years such were offered to her, and now she has the full certitude that our present globe and its human races must have been born, grown and developed in this, and in no other way."[158]

"The human Races are born one from the other, grow, develop, become old, and die. Their sub-races and nations follow the same rule."[159]

---

[158] *Ibid.*, p. 437-438
[159] *Ibid.*, p. 443-444

"No disbeliever who takes the 'Secret Doctrine' for a 'hoax' is forced or even asked to credit our statements..."

"Nor, is it after all, necessary that any one should believe in the Occult Sciences and the old teachings, before one knows anything or even believes in his own soul. No great truth was ever accepted a priori, and generally a century or two passed before it began to glimmer in the human consciousness as a possible verity, except in such cases as the positive discovery of the thing claimed as a fact. The truths of today are the falsehoods and errors of yesterday, and vice versa. It is only in the XXth century that portions, if not the whole, of the present work will be vindicated."

"We bide our time."[160]

[160] The Secret Doctrine, Vol. 2, p. 442

A prophecy about the Sixth Race

*"**S**ince the beginning of the Atlantean Race many million years have passed, yet we find the last of the Atlanteans, still mixed up with the Aryan element, 11,000 years ago. This shows the enormous overlapping of one race over the race which succeeds it, though in character and external type the elder loses its characteristics, and assumes the new features of the younger race. This is proved in all the formations of mixed human races. Now, Occult philosophy teaches that even now, under our very eyes, the new Race and Races are preparing to be formed, and that it is in America that the transformation will take place, and has already silently commenced.*

"Thus the Americans have become in only three centuries a 'primary race,' pro tem., before becoming a race apart, and strongly separated from all other now existing races. They are, in short, the germs of the Sixth sub-race, and in some few hundred years more, will become most decidedly the pioneers of that race which must succeed to the present European or fifth sub-race, in all its new characteristics. After this, in about 25,000 years, they will launch into preparations for the seventh sub-race; until, in consequence of cataclysms – the first series of those which must one day destroy Europe, and still later the whole Aryan race (and thus affect both Americas), as also most of the lands directly connected with the confines of our continent and isles – the Sixth Root-Race will have appeared on the stage of our Round. When shall this be? Who knows save the great Masters of Wisdom, perchance, and they are as silent upon the subject as the snow-capped peaks that tower

above them. All we know is, that it will silently come into existence; so silently, indeed, that for long millenniums shall its pioneers – the peculiar children who will grow into peculiar men and women – be regarded as anomalous lusus naturae, abnormal oddities physically and mentally. Then, as they increase, and their numbers become with every age greater, one day they will awake to find themselves in a majority. It is the present men who will then begin to be regarded as exceptional mongrels, until these die out in their turn in civilised lands; surviving only in small groups on islands – the mountain peaks of to-day – where they will vegetate, degenerate, and finally die out, perhaps millions of years hence, as the Aztecs have, as the Nyam-Nyam and the dwarfish Moola Koorumba of the Nilghiri Hills are dying. All these are the remnants of once mighty races, the recollection of whose existence has entirely died out of the remembrance of the modern generations, just as we shall vanish from the memory of the Sixth Race Humanity. The Fifth will overlap the Sixth Race for many hundreds of millenniums, changing with it slower than its new successor, still changing in stature, general physique, and mentality, just as the Fourth overlapped our Aryan race, and the Third had overlapped the Atlanteans.

"This process of preparation for the Sixth great Race must last throughout the whole sixth and seventh sub-races.[161] But the last remnants of the Fifth Continent will not disappear until some time after the birth of the new Race; when another and new dwelling, the sixth continent, will have appeared above the new waters on the face of the globe, so as to receive the new stranger. To it also will emigrate and

---

[161] Vide supra, the diagram of the Genealogical Tree of the Fifth Race.

110

settle all those who shall be fortunate enough to escape the general disaster. When this shall be – as just said – it is not for the writer to know. Only, as nature no more proceeds by sudden jumps and starts, than man changes suddenly from a child into a mature man, the final cataclysm will be preceded by many smaller submersions and destructions both by wave and volcanic fires. The exultant pulse will beat high in the heart of the race now in the American zone, but there will be no more Americans when the Sixth Race commences; no more, in fact, than Europeans; for they will have now become a new race, and many new nations. Yet the Fifth will not die, but survive for a while: overlapping the new Race for many hundred thousands of years to come, it will become transformed with it – slower than its new successor – still getting entirely altered in mentality, general physique, and stature. Mankind will not grow again into giant bodies as in the case of the Lemurians and the Atlanteans; because while the evolution of the Fourth race led the latter down to the very bottom of materiality in its physical development, the present Race is on its ascending arc; and the Sixth will be rapidly growing out of its bonds of matter, and even of flesh.

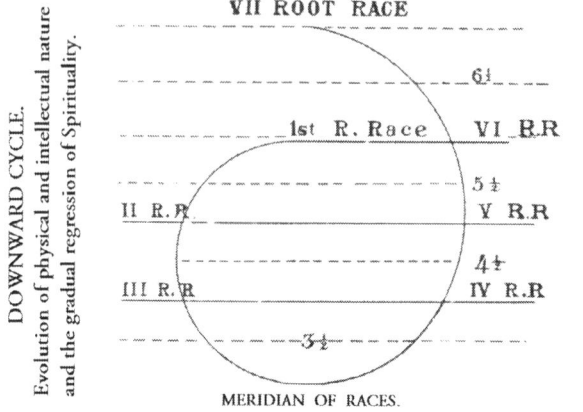

"Thus it is the mankind of the New world – one by far the senior of our Old one, a fact men had also forgotten – of Patala (the Antipodes, or the Nether World, as America is called in India), whose mission and Karma it is, to sow the seeds for a forthcoming, grander, and far more glorious Race than any of those we know of at present.

"The Cycles of Matter will be succeeded by Cycles of Spirituality and a fully developed mind. On the law of parallel history and races, the majority of the future mankind will be composed of glorious Adepts. Humanity is the child of cyclic Destiny, and not one of its Units can escape its unconscious mission, or get rid of the burden of its co-operative work with nature. Thus will mankind, race after race, perform its appointed cycle-pilgrimage. Climates will, and have already begun, to change, each tropical year after the other dropping one sub-race, but only to beget another higher race on the ascending cycle; while a series of other less favoured groups – the failures of nature –

will, like some individual men, vanish from the human family without even leaving a trace behind. Such is the course of Nature under the sway of KARMIC LAW: of the ever present and the ever-becoming Nature. "[162]

---

[162] The Secret Doctrine, Vol. 2, p. 444-446

One more digression from the subject

Before we turn to how *The Secret Doctrine* treats the meaning of the war in Heaven, in order to make this subject more understandable, I suggest that you become acquainted with the historical document called *The Apocryphon of John*[163]. It is a rather hefty document, yet I am asking you to read it or at least to understand the general contents of this document. I will also make an attempt to give my commentary to this document below, basing it on the Spirit of *The Secret Doctrine*.

The Apocryphon of John

The teaching of the savior, and the revelation of the mysteries and the things hidden in silence, even these things which he taught John, his disciple.

And it happened one day, when John, the brother of James – who are the sons of Zebedee – had come up to the temple, that a Pharisee named Arimanius approached him and said to him, "Where is your master whom you followed?" And he said to him, "He has gone to the place from which he came." The Pharisee said to him, "With deception did this Nazarene deceive you (pl.), and he filled your ears with lies, and closed

---

[163] Translated by Frederik Wisse. *The Apocryphon of John* is commonly referenced by two other names: *The Secret Book of John* and *The Secret Revelation of John*, depending upon how the word "Apocryphon" is translated. There are four surviving Coptic manuscripts of this text: two shorter versions found in the Berlin Codex and Nag Hammadi Codex III, and two longer versions, found in Nag Hammadi Codex II and IV. This translation prepared by Dr. Wisse for the Nag Hammadi Library in English uses all four manuscripts to produce a single text.

Separate translations of the short and long versions, along with extensive additional resources, are available in the *Apocryphon of John Collection* of the Gnostic Society Library: http://www.gnosis.org/naghamm/nhl_sbj.htm

your hearts (and) turned you from the traditions of your fathers."

When I, John, heard these things I turned away from the temple to a desert place. And I grieved greatly in my heart, saying, "How then was the savior appointed, and why was he sent into the world by his Father, and who is his Father who sent him, and of what sort is that aeon[164] to which we shall go? For what did he mean when he said to us, 'This aeon to which you will go is of the type of the imperishable aeon, but he did not teach us concerning the latter, of what sort it is."

Straightway, while I was contemplating these things, behold, the heavens opened and the whole creation which is below heaven shone, and the world was shaken. I was afraid, and behold I saw in the light a youth who stood by me. While I looked at him, he became like an old man. And he changed his likeness (again), becoming like a servant. There was not a plurality before me, but there was a likeness with multiple forms in the light, and the likenesses appeared through each other, and the likeness had three forms.

He said to me, "John, John, why do you doubt, or why are you afraid? You are not unfamiliar with this image, are you? – that is, do not be timid! – I am the one who is with you (pl.) always. I am the Father, I am the Mother, I am the Son. I am the undefiled and incorruptible one. Now I have come to teach you what is and what was and what will come to pass, that you may know the things which are not revealed and those which are revealed, and to teach you concerning the unwavering race of the perfect Man. Now, therefore, lift up your face, that you may receive the things that I

---

[164] **Æon** or **Æons** (*Gr.*). Periods of time; emanations proceeding from the divine essence, and celestial beings; genii and angels with the Gnostics. (The Theosophical Glossary by H.P. Blavatsky)

shall teach you today, and may tell them to your fellow spirits who are from the unwavering race of the perfect Man."

And I asked to know it, and he said to me, "The Monad is a monarchy with nothing above it. It is he who exists as God and Father of everything, the invisible One who is above everything, who exists as incorruption, which is in the pure light into which no eye can look.

"He is the invisible Spirit, of whom it is not right to think of him as a god, or something similar. For he is more than a god, since there is nothing above him, for no one lords it over him. For he does not exist in something inferior to him, since everything exists in him. For it is he who establishes himself. He is eternal, since he does not need anything. For he is total perfection. He did not lack anything, that he might be completed by it; rather he is always completely perfect in light. He is illimitable, since there is no one prior to him to set limits to him. He is unsearchable, since there exists no one prior to him to examine him. He is immeasurable, since there was no one prior to him to measure him. He is invisible, since no one saw him. He is eternal, since he exists eternally. He is ineffable, since no one was able to comprehend him to speak about him. He is unnameable, since there is no one prior to him to give him a name.

"He is immeasurable light, which is pure, holy (and) immaculate. He is ineffable, being perfect in incorruptibility. (He is) not in perfection, nor in blessedness, nor in divinity, but he is far superior. He is not corporeal nor is he incorporeal. He is neither large nor is he small. There is no way to say, 'What is his quantity?' or, 'What is his quality?', for no one can know him. He is not someone among (other) beings, rather he is far superior. Not that he is (simply) superior, but his essence does not partake in the aeons nor in time. For he who partakes in an aeon was prepared beforehand. Time was not apportioned to him, since he does not receive anything from another, for it would be received on loan. For he who precedes someone does not lack, that he may receive from him. For rather, it is the latter that looks expectantly at him in his light.

"For the perfection is majestic. He is pure, immeasurable mind. He is an aeon-giving aeon. He is life-giving life. He is a blessedness-giving blessed one. He is knowledge-giving knowledge. He is goodness-giving goodness. He is mercy and redemption-giving mercy. He is grace-giving grace, not because he possesses it, but because he gives the immeasurable, incomprehensible light.

"How am I to speak with you about him? His aeon is indestructible, at rest and existing in silence, reposing (and) being prior to everything. For he is the head of all the aeons, and it is he who gives them strength in his goodness. For we know not the ineffable things, and we do not understand what is immeasurable, except for him who came forth from him, namely (from) the Father. For it is he who told it to us alone. For it is he who looks at himself in his light which surrounds him, namely the spring of the water of life. And it is he who gives to all the aeons and in every way, (and) who gazes upon his image which he sees in the spring of the Spirit. It is he who puts his desire in his water-light which is in the spring of the pure light-water which surrounds him.

"And his thought performed a deed and she came forth, namely she who had appeared before him in the shine of his light. This is the first power which was before all of them (and) which came forth from his mind, She is the forethought of the All – her light shines like his light – the perfect power which is the image of the invisible, virginal Spirit who is perfect. The first power, the glory of Barbelo, the perfect glory in the aeons, the glory of the revelation, she glorified the virginal Spirit and it was she who praised him, because thanks to him she had come forth. This is the first thought, his image; she became the womb of everything, for it is she who is prior to them all, the Mother-Father, the first man, the holy Spirit, the thrice-male, the thrice-powerful, the thrice-named androgynous one, and the eternal aeon among the invisible ones, and the first to come forth.

"<She> requested from the invisible, virginal Spirit – that is Barbelo – to give her foreknowledge. And the Spirit consented. And when he had consented, the foreknowledge came forth, and it stood by the forethought; it originates from the thought of the invisible, virginal Spirit. It glorified him and his perfect power, Barbelo, for it was for her sake that it had come into being.

"And she requested again to grant her indestructibility, and he consented. When he had consented, indestructibility came forth, and it stood by the thought and the foreknowledge. It glorified the invisible One and Barbelo, the one for whose sake they had come into being.

"And Barbelo requested to grant her eternal life. And the invisible Spirit consented. And when he had consented, eternal life came forth, and they attended and glorified the invisible Spirit and Barbelo, the one for whose sake they had come into being.

"And she requested again to grant her truth. And the invisible Spirit consented. And when he had consented, truth came forth, and they attended and glorified the invisible, excellent Spirit and his Barbelo, the one for whose sake they had come into being.

"This is the pentad of the aeons of the Father, which is the first man, the image of the invisible Spirit; it is the forethought, which Barbelo, and the thought, and the foreknowledge, and the indestructibility, and the eternal life, and the truth. This is the androgynous pentad of the aeons, which is the decad of the aeons, which is the Father.

"And he looked at Barbelo with the pure light which surrounds the invisible Spirit, and (with) his spark, and she conceived from him. He begot a spark of light with a light resembling blessedness. But it does not equal his greatness. This was an only-begotten child of the Mother-Father which had come forth; it is the only offspring, the only-begotten one of the Father, the pure Light.

"And the invisible, virginal Spirit rejoiced over the light which came forth, that which was brought forth first by the first power of his forethought, which is Barbelo. And he anointed it with his goodness until it became perfect, not lacking in any goodness, because he had anointed it with the goodness of the invisible Spirit. And it attended him as he poured upon it. And immediately when it had received from the Spirit, it glorified the holy Spirit and the perfect forethought, for whose sake it had come forth.

"And it requested to give it a fellow worker, which is the mind, and he consented gladly. And when the invisible Spirit had consented, the mind came forth, and it attended Christ, glorifying him and Barbelo. And all these came into being in silence.

"And the mind wanted to perform a deed through the word of the invisible Spirit. And his will became a deed and it appeared with the mind; and the light glorified it. And the word followed the will. For because of the word, Christ the divine Autogenes created everything. And the eternal life <and> his will and the mind and the foreknowledge attended and glorified the invisible Spirit and Barbelo, for whose sake they had come into being.

"And the holy Spirit completed the divine Autogenes, his son, together with Barbelo, that he may attend the mighty and invisible, virginal Spirit as the divine Autogenes, the Christ whom he had honored with a mighty voice. He came forth through the forethought. And the invisible, virginal Spirit placed the divine Autogenes of truth over everything. And he subjected to him every authority, and the truth which is in him, that he may know the All which had been called with a name exalted above every name. For that name will be mentioned to those who are worthy of it.

"For from the light, which is the Christ, and the indestructibility, through the gift of the Spirit the four lights (appeared) from the divine Autogenes. He expected that they might attend him. And the three (are) will, thought, and life. And the four powers (are) understanding, grace, perception, and prudence. And grace belongs to the light-aeon Armozel, which is the first angel. And there are three other aeons with this aeon: grace, truth, and form. And the second light (is) Oriel, who has been placed over the second aeon. And there are three other aeons with him: conception, perception, and memory. And the third light is Daveithai, who has been placed over the third aeon. And there are three other aeons with him: understanding, love, and idea. And the fourth aeon was placed over the fourth light Eleleth. And there are three other aeons with him: perfection, peace, and wisdom.

These are the four lights which attend the divine Autogenes, (and) these are the twelve aeons which attend the son of the mighty one, the Autogenes, the Christ, through the will and the gift of the invisible Spirit. And the twelve aeons belong to the son of the Autogenes. And all things were established by the will of the holy Spirit through the Autogenes.

"And from the foreknowledge of the perfect mind, through the revelation of the will of the invisible Spirit and the will of the Autogenes, <the> perfect Man (appeared), the first revelation, and the truth. It is he whom the virginal Spirit called Pigera-Adamas, and he placed him over the first aeon with the mighty one, the Autogenes, the Christ, by the first light Armozel; and with him are his powers. And the invisible one gave him a spiritual, invincible power. And he spoke and glorified and praised the invisible Spirit, saying, 'It is for thy sake that everything has come into being and everything will return to thee. I shall praise and glorify thee and the Autogenes and the aeons, the three: the Father, the Mother, and the Son, the perfect power.'

"And he placed his son Seth over the second aeon in the presence of the second light Oriel. And in the third aeon the seed of Seth was placed over the third light Daveithai. And the souls of the saints were placed (there). And in the fourth aeon the souls were placed of those who do not know the Pleroma and who did not repent at once, but who persisted for a while and repented afterwards; they are by the fourth light Eleleth. These are creatures which glorify the invisible Spirit.

"And the Sophia of the Epinoia[165], being an aeon, conceived a thought from herself and the conception of

---

[165] **Epinoia** (*Gr.*). Thought, invention, design. A name adopted by the Gnostics for the first passive Æon. (The Theosophical Glossary by H.P. Blavatsky)

the invisible Spirit and foreknowledge. She wanted to bring forth a likeness out of herself without the consent of the Spirit, – he had not approved – and without her consort, and without his consideration. And though the person of her maleness had not approved, and she had not found her agreement, and she had thought without the consent of the Spirit and the knowledge of her agreement, (yet) she brought forth. And because of the invincible power which is in her, her thought did not remain idle, and something came out of her which was imperfect and different from her appearance, because she had created it without her consort. And it was dissimilar to the likeness of its mother, for it has another form.

"And when she saw (the consequences of) her desire, it changed into a form of a lion-faced serpent. And its eyes were like lightning fires which flash. She cast it away from her, outside that place, that no one of the immortal ones might see it, for she had created it in ignorance. And she surrounded it with a luminous cloud, and she placed a throne in the middle of the cloud that no one might see it except the holy Spirit who is called the mother of the living. And she called his name Yaltabaoth[166].

"This is the first archon who took a great power from his mother. And he removed himself from her and

---

[166] **Ilda Baoth.** *Lit.*, "the child from the Egg", a Gnostic term. He is the creator of our physical globe (the earth) according to the Gnostic teaching in the *Codex Nazaræus* (the Evangel of the Nazarenes and the Ebionites). The latter identifies him with Jehovah the God of the Jews. Ildabaoth is "the Son of Darkness" in a bad sense and the father of the six terrestrial "Stellar", dark spirits, the antithesis of the bright Stellar spirits. Their respective abodes are the seven spheres, the upper of which begins in the "middle space", the region of their mother Sophia Achamôth, and the lower ending on this earth – the seventh region (See *Isis Unveiled*, Vol. II., 183.) Ilda-Baoth is the genius of Saturn, the planet; or rather the evil spirit of its ruler. (The Theosophical Glossary by H.P. Blavatsky)

moved away from the places in which he was born. He became strong and created for himself other aeons with a flame of luminous fire which (still) exists now. And he joined with his arrogance which is in him and begot authorities for himself. The name of the first one is Athoth, whom the generations call the reaper. The second one is Harmas, who is the eye of envy. The third one is Kalila-Oumbri. The fourth one is Yabel. The fifth one is Adonaiou, who is called Sabaoth. The sixth one is Cain, whom the generations of men call the sun. The seventh is Abel. The eighth is Abrisene. The ninth is Yobel. The tenth is Armoupieel. The eleventh is Melceir-Adonein. The twelfth is Belias, it is he who is over the depth of Hades. And he placed seven kings – each corresponding to the firmaments of heaven – over the seven heavens, and five over the depth of the abyss, that they may reign. And he shared his fire with them, but he did not send forth from the power of the light which he had taken from his mother, for he is ignorant darkness.

"And when the light had mixed with the darkness, it caused the darkness to shine. And when the darkness had mixed with the light, it darkened the light and it became neither light nor dark, but it became dim.

"Now the archon who is weak has three names. The first name is Yaltabaoth, the second is Saklas, and the third is Samael. And he is impious in his arrogance which is in him. For he said, 'I am God and there is no other God beside me,' for he is ignorant of his strength, the place from which he had come.

"And the archons created seven powers for themselves, and the powers created for themselves six angels for each one until they became 365 angels. And these are the bodies belonging with the names: the first is Athoth, a he has a sheep's face; the second is Eloaiou, he has a donkey's face; the third is Astaphaios, he has a hyena's face; the fourth is Yao, he has a serpent's face with seven heads; the fifth is Sabaoth, he has a dragon's face; the sixth is Adonin, he had a monkey's face; the seventh is Sabbede, he has a shining fire-face. This is the sevenness of the week.

"But Yaltabaoth had a multitude of faces, more than all of them, so that he could put a face before all of them, according to his desire, when he is in the midst of seraphs. He shared his fire with them; therefore he became lord over them. Because of the power of the glory he possessed of his mother's light, he called himself God. And he did not obey the place from which he came. And he united the seven powers in his thought with the authorities which were with him. And when he spoke it happened. And he named each power beginning with the highest: the first is goodness with the first (authority), Athoth; the second is foreknowledge with the second one, Eloaio; and the third is divinity with the third one, Astraphaio); the fourth is lordship with the fourth one, Yao; the fifth is kingdom with the fifth one, Sabaoth; the sixth is envy with the sixth one, Adonein; the seventh is understanding with the seventh one, Sabbateon. And these have a firmament corresponding to each aeon-heaven. They were given names according to the glory which belongs to heaven for the destruction of the powers. And in the names which were given to them by their Originator there was power. But the names which were given them according to the glory which belongs to heaven mean for them destruction and powerlessness. Thus they have two names.

"And having created [...] everything, he organized according to the model of the first aeons which had come into being, so that he might create them like the indestructible ones. Not because he had seen the indestructible ones, but the power in him, which he had taken from his mother, produced in him the likeness of the cosmos. And when he saw the creation which surrounds him, and the multitude of the angels around him which had come forth from him, he said to them, 'I am a jealous God, and there is no other God beside me.' But by announcing this he indicated to the angels who attended him that there exists another God. For if there were no other one, of whom would he be jealous?

"Then the mother began to move to and fro. She became aware of the deficiency when the brightness of her light diminished. And she became dark because her consort had not agreed with her."

And I said, "Lord, what does it mean that she moved to and fro?" But he smiled and said, "Do not think it is, as Moses said, 'above the waters.' No, but when she had seen the wickedness which had happened, and the theft which her son had committed, she repented. And she was overcome by forgetfulness in the darkness of ignorance and she began to be ashamed. And she did not dare to return, but she was moving about. And the moving is the going to and fro.

"And the arrogant one took a power from his mother. For he was ignorant, thinking that there existed no other except his mother alone. And when he saw the multitude of the angels which he had created, then he exalted himself above them.

"And when the mother recognized that the garment of darkness was imperfect, then she knew that her consort had not agreed with her. She repented with much weeping. And the whole pleroma[167] heard the

---

[167] **Pleroma** (*Gr.*). "Fulness", a Gnostic term adopted to signify the divine world or Universal Soul. Space, developed and divided into a series of

prayer of her repentance, and they praised on her behalf the invisible, virginal Spirit. And he consented; and when the invisible Spirit had consented, the holy Spirit poured over her from their whole pleroma. For it was not her consort who came to her, but he came to her through the pleroma in order that he might correct her deficiency. And she was taken up not to her own aeon but above her son, that she might be in the ninth until she has corrected her deficiency.

"And a voice came forth from the exalted aeon-heaven: 'The Man exists and the son of Man.' And the chief archon, Yaltabaoth, heard (it) and thought that the voice had come from his mother. And he did not know from where it came. And he taught them, the holy and perfect Mother-Father, the complete foreknowledge, the image of the invisible one who is the Father of the all (and) through whom everything came into being, the first Man. For he revealed his likeness in a human form.

"And the whole aeon of the chief archon trembled, and the foundations of the abyss shook. And of the waters which are above matter, the underside was illuminated by the appearance of his image which had been revealed. And when all the authorities and the chief archon looked, they saw the whole region of the underside which was illuminated. And through the light they saw the form of the image in the water.

"And he said to the authorities which attend him, 'Come, let us create a man according to the image of God and according to our likeness, that his image may become a light for us.' And they created by means of their respective powers in correspondence with the characteristics which were given. And each authority supplied a characteristic in the form of the image which

---

æons. The abode of the invisible gods. It has three degrees. (The Theosophical Glossary by H.P. Blavatsky)

he had seen in its natural (form). He created a being according to the likeness of the first, perfect Man. And they said, 'Let us call him Adam, that his name may become a power of light for us.'

"And the powers began: the first one, goodness, created a bone-soul; and the second, foreknowledge, created a sinew-soul; the third, divinity, created a flesh-soul; and the fourth, the lordship, created a marrow-soul; the fifth, kingdom created a blood-soul; the sixth, envy, created a skin-soul; the seventh, understanding, created a hair-soul. And the multitude of the angels attended him and they received from the powers the seven substances of the natural (form) in order to create the proportions of the limbs and the proportion of the rump and the proper working together of each of the parts.

"The first one began to create the head. Eteraphaope-Abron created his head; Meniggesstroeth created the brain; Asterechme (created) the right eye; Thaspomocha, the left eye; Yeronumos, the right ear; Bissoum, the left ear; Akioreim, the nose; Banen-Ephroum, the lips; Amen, the teeth; Ibikan, the molars; Basiliademe, the tonsils; Achcha, the uvula; Adaban, the neck; Chaaman, the vertebrae; Dearcho, the throat; Tebar, the right shoulder; [...], the left shoulder; Mniarcon, the right elbow; [...], the left elbow; Abitrion, the right underarm; Evanthen, the left underarm; Krys, the right hand; Beluai, the left hand; Treneu, the fingers of the right hand; Balbel, the fingers of the left hand; Kriman, the nails of the hands; Astrops, the right breast; Barroph, the left breast; Baoum, the right shoulder joint; Ararim, the left shoulder joint; Areche, the belly; Phthave, the navel; Senaphim, the abdomen; Arachethopi, the right ribs; Zabedo, the left ribs; Barias, the right hip; Phnouth the left hip; Abenlenarchei, the marrow; Chnoumeninorin, the bones; Gesole, the stomach; Agromauna, the heart; Bano, the lungs; Sostrapal, the liver; Anesimalar, the spleen; Thopithro, the intestines; Biblo, the kidneys; Roeror, the sinews; Taphreo, the spine of the body; Ipouspoboba, the veins; Bineborin, the arteries; Atoimenpsephei, theirs are the breaths which are in all the limbs; Entholleia, all the flesh; Bedouk, the right buttock (?); Arabeei, the left penis; Eilo, the testicles; Sorma, the genitals; Gorma-Kaiochlabar, the right thigh; Nebrith, the left thigh; Pserem, the kidneys of the right leg; Asaklas, the left kidney; Ormaoth, the right leg; Emenun, the left leg; Knyx, the right shin-bone; Tupelon, the left shin-bone; Achiel, the right knee; Phnene, the left knee; Phiouthrom, the right foot; Boabel, its toes; Trachoun, the left foot; Phikna, its toes; Miamai, the nails of the feet; Labernioum – .

"And those who were appointed over all of these are: Zathoth, Armas, Kalila, Jabel, (Sabaoth, Cain, Abel). And those who are particularly active in the limbs (are) the head Diolimodraza, the neck Yammeax, the right shoulder Yakouib, the left shoulder Verton, the right hand Oudidi, the left one Arbao, the fingers of the right hand Lampno, the fingers of the left hand Leekaphar, the right breast Barbar, the left breast Imae, the chest Pisandriaptes, the right shoulder joint Koade, the left shoulder joint Odeor, the right ribs Asphixix, the left ribs Synogchouta, the belly Arouph, the womb Sabalo, the right thigh Charcharb, the left thigh Chthaon, all the genitals Bathinoth, the right leg Choux, the left leg Charcha, the right shin-bone Aroer, the left shin-bone Toechtha, the right knee Aol, the left knee Charaner, the right foot Bastan, its toes Archentechtha, the left foot Marephnounth, its toes Abrana.

"Seven have power over all of these: Michael, Ouriel, Asmenedas, Saphasatoel, Aarmouriam, Richram, Amiorps. And the ones who are in charge over the senses (are) Archendekta; and he who is in charge over the receptions (is) Deitharbathas; and he who is in charge over the imagination (is) Oummaa; and he who is over the composition Aachiaram, and he who is over the whole impulse Riaramnacho.

"And the origin of the demons which are in the whole body is determined to be four: heat, cold, wetness, and dryness. And the mother of all of them is matter. And he who reigns over the heat (is) Phloxopha; and he who reigns over the cold is Oroorrothos; and he who reigns over what is dry (is) Erimacho; and he who reigns over the wetness (is) Athuro. And the mother of all of these, Onorthochrasaei, stands in their midst, since she is illimitable, and she mixes with all of them. And she is truly matter, for they are nourished by her.

"The four chief demons are: Ephememphi, who belongs to pleasure, Yoko, who belongs to desire, Nenentophni, who belongs to grief, Blaomen, who belongs to fear. And the mother of them all is Aesthesis-Ouch-Epi-Ptoe. And from the four demons passions came forth. And from grief (came) envy, jealousy, distress, trouble, pain, callousness, anxiety, mourning, etc. And from pleasure much wickedness arises, and empty pride, and similar things. And from desire (comes) anger, wrath, and bitterness, and bitter passion, and unsatedness, and similar things. And from fear (comes) dread, fawning, agony, and shame. All of these are like useful things as well as evil things. But the insight into their true (character) is Anaro, who is the head of the material soul, for it belongs with the seven senses, Ouch-Epi-Ptoe.

"This is the number of the angels: together they are 365. They all worked on it until, limb for limb, the natural and the material body was completed by them. Now there are other ones in charge over the remaining passions whom I did not mention to you. But if you wish to know them, it is written in the book of Zoroaster. And all the angels and demons worked until they had constructed the natural body. And their product was completely inactive and motionless for a long time.

"And when the mother wanted to retrieve the power which she had given to the chief archon, she petitioned the Mother-Father of the All, who is most merciful. He sent, by means of the holy decree, the five lights down upon the place of the angels of the chief archon. They advised him that they should bring forth the power of the mother. And they said to Yaltabaoth, 'Blow into his face something of your spirit and his body will arise.' And he blew into his face the spirit which is the power of his mother; he did not know (this), for he exists in ignorance. And the power of the mother went out of Yaltabaoth into the natural body, which they had fashioned after the image of the one who exists from the beginning. The body moved and gained strength, and it was luminous.

"And in that moment the rest of the powers became jealous, because he had come into being through all of them and they had given their power to the man, and his intelligence was greater than that of those who had made him, and greater than that of the chief archon. And when they recognized that he was luminous, and that he could think better than they, and that he was free from wickedness, they took him and threw him into the lowest region of all matter.

"But the blessed One, the Mother-Father, the beneficent and merciful One, had mercy on the power of the mother which had been brought forth out of the chief archon, for they (the archons) might gain power over the natural and perceptible body. And he sent, through his beneficent Spirit and his great mercy, a helper to Adam, luminous Epinoia which comes out of him, who is called Life. And she assists the whole creature, by toiling with him and by restoring him to his fullness and by teaching him about the descent of his seed (and) by teaching him about the way of ascent, (which is) the way he came down. And the luminous Epinoia was hidden in Adam, in order that the archons might not know her, but that the Epinoia might be a correction of the deficiency of the mother.

"And the man came forth because of the shadow of the light which is in him. And his thinking was superior to all those who had made him. When they looked up, they saw that his thinking was superior. And they took counsel with the whole array of archons and angels. They took fire and earth and water and mixed them together with the four fiery winds. And they wrought them together and caused a great disturbance. And they brought him (Adam) into the shadow of death, in order that they might form (him) again from earth and water and fire and the spirit which originates in matter, which is the ignorance of darkness and desire, and their counterfeit spirit. This is the tomb of the newly-formed body with which the robbers had clothed the man, the bond of forgetfulness; and he became a mortal man. This is the first one who came down, and the first separation. But the Epinoia of the light which was in him, she is the one who was to awaken his thinking.

"And the archons took him and placed him in paradise. And they said to him, 'Eat, that is at leisure,' for their luxury is bitter and their beauty is depraved. And their luxury is deception and their trees are godlessness and their fruit is deadly poison and their promise is death. And the tree of their life they had placed in the midst of paradise.

"And I shall teach you (pl.) what is the mystery of their life, which is the plan which they made together, which is the likeness of their spirit. The root of this (tree) is bitter and its branches are death, its shadow is hate and deception is in its leaves, and its blossom is the ointment of evil, and its fruit is death and desire is its seed, and it sprouts in darkness. The dwelling place of those who taste from it is Hades, and the darkness is their place of rest.

"But what they call the tree of knowledge of good and evil, which is the Epinoia of the light, they stayed in front of it in order that he (Adam) might not look up to his fullness and recognize the nakedness of his shamefulness. But it was I who brought about that they ate."

And to I said to the savior, "Lord, was it not the serpent that taught Adam to eat?" The savior smiled and said, "The serpent taught them to eat from wickedness of begetting, lust, (and) destruction, that he (Adam) might be useful to him. And he (Adam) knew that he was disobedient to him (the chief archon) due to light of the Epinoia which is in him, which made him more correct in his thinking than the chief archon. And (the latter) wanted to bring about the power which he himself had given him. And he brought a forgetfulness over Adam."

And I said to the savior, "What is the forgetfulness?" And he said "It is not the way Moses wrote (and) you heard. For he said in his first book, 'He put him to sleep' (Gn 2:21), but (it was) in his perception. For also he said through the prophet, 'I will make their hearts heavy, that they may not pay attention and may not see' (Is 6:10).

"Then the Epinoia of the light hid herself in him (Adam). And the chief archon wanted to bring her out of his rib. But the Epinoia of the light cannot be grasped. Although darkness pursued her, it did not catch her. And he brought a part of his power out of him. And he made another creature, in the form of a woman, according to the likeness of the Epinoia which had appeared to him. And he brought the part which he had taken from the power of the man into the female creature, and not as Moses said, 'his rib-bone.'

"And he (Adam) saw the woman beside him. And in that moment the luminous Epinoia appeared, and she lifted the veil which lay over his mind. And he became sober from the drunkenness of darkness. And he recognized his counter-image, and he said, 'This is indeed bone of my bones and flesh of my flesh.' Therefore the man will leave his father and his mother, and he will cleave to his wife, and they will both be one flesh. For they will send him his consort, and he will leave his father and his mother ... (3 lines unreadable)

"And our sister Sophia (is) she who came down in innocence in order to rectify her deficiency. Therefore she was called Life, which is the mother of the living, by the foreknowledge of the sovereignty of heaven. And through her they have tasted the perfect Knowledge. I appeared in the form of an eagle on the tree of knowledge, which is the Epinoia from the foreknowledge of the pure light, that I might teach them and awaken them out of the depth of sleep. For they were both in a fallen state, and they recognized their nakedness. The Epinoia appeared to them as a light; she awakened their thinking.

"And when Yaltabaoth noticed that they withdrew from him, he cursed his earth. He found the woman as she was preparing herself for her husband. He was lord over her, though he did not know the mystery which had come to pass through the holy decree. And they were afraid to blame him. And he showed his angels his ignorance which is in him. And he cast them out of paradise and he clothed them in gloomy darkness. And the chief archon saw the virgin who stood by Adam, and that the luminous Epinoia of life had appeared in her. And Yaltabaoth was full of ignorance. And when the foreknowledge of the All noticed (it), she sent some and they snatched life out of Eve.

"And the chief archon seduced her and he begot in her two sons; the first and the second (are) Eloim and Yave. Eloim has a bear-face and Yave has a cat-face. The one is righteous but the other is unrighteous. (Yave is righteous but Eloim is unrighteous.) Yave he set over the fire and the wind, and Eloim he set over the water and the earth. And these he called with the names Cain and Abel with a view to deceive.

"Now up to the present day, sexual intercourse continued due to the chief archon. And he planted sexual desire in her who belongs to Adam. And he produced through intercourse the copies of the bodies, and he inspired them with his counterfeit spirit.

"And the two archons he set over principalities, so that they might rule over the tomb. And when Adam recognized the likeness of his own foreknowledge, he begot the likeness of the son of man. He called him Seth, according to the way of the race in the aeons. Likewise, the mother also sent down her spirit, which is in her likeness and a copy of those who are in the pleroma, for she will prepare a dwelling place for the aeons which will come down. And he made them drink water of forgetfulness, from the chief archon, in order that they might not know from where they came. Thus, the seed remained for a while assisting (him), in order that, when the Spirit comes forth from the holy aeons, he may raise up and heal him from the deficiency, that the whole pleroma may (again) become holy and faultless."

And I said to the savior, "Lord, will all the souls then be brought safely into the pure light?" He answered and said to me, "Great things have arisen in your mind, for it is difficult to explain them to others except to those who are from the immovable race. Those on whom the Spirit of life will descend and (with whom) he will be with the power, they will be saved and become perfect and be worthy of the greatness and be purified in that place from all wickedness and the involvements in evil. Then they have no other care than the incorruption alone, to which they direct their attention from here on, without anger or envy or jealousy or desire and greed of anything. They are not affected by anything except the state of being in the flesh alone, which they bear while looking expectantly for the time when they will be met by the receivers (of the body). Such then are worthy of the imperishable, eternal life and the calling. For they endure everything and bear up under everything, that they may finish the good fight and inherit eternal life."

I said to him, "Lord, the souls of those who did not do these works (but) on whom the power and Spirit descended, will they be rejected?" He answered and said to me, "If the Spirit (descended upon them), they will in any case be saved, and they will change (for the better). For the power will descend on every man, for without it no one can stand. And after they are born, then, when the Spirit of life increases and the power comes and strengthens that soul, no one can lead it astray with works of evil. But those on whom the counterfeit spirit descends are drawn by him and they go astray."

And I said, "Lord, where will the souls of these go when they have come out of their flesh?" And he smiled and said to me, "The soul in which the power will become stronger than the counterfeit spirit, is strong and it flees from evil and, through the intervention of the incorruptible one, it is saved, and it is taken up to the rest of the aeons."

And I said, "Lord, those, however, who have not known to whom they belong, where will their souls be?" And he said to me, "In those, the despicable spirit has gained strength when they went astray. And he burdens the soul and draws it to the works of evil, and he casts it down into forgetfulness. And after it comes out of (the body), it is handed over to the authorities, who came into being through the archon, and they bind it with chains and cast it into prison, and consort with it until it is liberated from the forgetfulness and acquires knowledge. And if thus it becomes perfect, it is saved."

And I said, "Lord, how can the soul become smaller and return into the nature of its mother or into man?" Then he rejoiced when I asked him this, and he said to me, "Truly, you are blessed, for you have understood! That soul is made to follow another one (fem.), since the Spirit of life is in it. It is saved through him. It is not again cast into another flesh."

And I said, "Lord, these also who did not know, but have turned away, where will their souls go?" Then he said to me, "To that place where the angels of poverty go they will be taken, the place where there is no repentance. And they will be kept for the day on which those who have blasphemed the spirit will be tortured, and they will be punished with eternal punishment."

And I said, "Lord, from where did the counterfeit spirit come?" Then he said to me, "The Mother-Father, who is rich in mercy, the holy Spirit in every way, the One who is merciful and who sympathizes with you (pl.), i.e., the Epinoia of the foreknowledge of light, he raised up the offspring of the perfect race and its thinking and the eternal light of man. When the chief archon realized that they were exalted above him in the height – and they surpass him in thinking – then he wanted to seize their thought, not knowing that they surpassed him in thinking, and that he will not be able to seize them.

"He made a plan with his authorities, which are his powers, and they committed together adultery with Sophia, and bitter fate was begotten through them, which is the last of the changeable bonds. And it is of a sort that is interchangeable. And it is harder and stronger than she with whom the gods united, and the angels and the demons and all the generations until this day. For from that fate came forth every sin and injustice and blasphemy, and the chain of forgetfulness and ignorance and every severe command, and serious sins and great fears. And thus the whole creation was made blind, in order that they may not know God, who is above all of them. And because of the chain of forgetfulness, their sins were hidden. For they are bound with measures and times and moments, since it (fate) is lord over everything.

"And he (the chief archon) repented for everything which had come into being through him. This time he planned to bring a flood upon the work of man. But the greatness of the light of the foreknowledge informed Noah, and he proclaimed (it) to all the offspring which are the sons of men. But those who were strangers to him did not listen to him. It is not as Moses said, 'They hid themselves in an ark' (Gn 7: 7), but they hid themselves in a place, not only Noah, but also many other people from the immovable race. They went into a place and hid themselves in a luminous cloud. And he (Noah) recognized his authority, and she who belongs to the light was with him, having shone on them because he (the chief archon) had brought darkness upon the whole earth.

"And he made a plan with his powers. He sent his angels to the daughters of men, that they might take some of them for themselves and raise offspring for their enjoyment. And at first they did not succeed. When they had no success, they gathered together again and they made a plan together. They created a counterfeit spirit, who resembles the Spirit who had descended, so as to pollute the souls through it. And the angels changed themselves in their likeness into the likeness of their mates (the daughters of men), filling them with the spirit of darkness, which they had mixed for them, and with evil. They brought gold and silver and a gift and copper and iron and metal and all kinds of things. And they steered the people who had followed them into great troubles, by leading them astray with many deceptions. They (the people) became old without having enjoyment. They died, not having found truth and without knowing the God of truth. And thus the whole creation became enslaved forever, from the foundation of the world until now. And they took women and begot children out of the darkness according to the likeness of their spirit. And they closed their hearts, and they hardened themselves through the hardness of the counterfeit spirit until now.

"I, therefore, the perfect Pronoia of the all, changed myself into my seed, for I existed first, going on every road. For I am the richness of the light; I am the remembrance of the pleroma.

"And I went into the realm of darkness and I endured till I entered the middle of the prison. And the foundations of chaos shook. And I hid myself from them because of their wickedness, and they did not recognize me.

"Again I returned for the second time, and I went about. I came forth from those who belong to the light, which is I, the remembrance of the Pronoia. I entered into the midst of darkness and the inside of Hades, since I was seeking (to accomplish) my task. And the foundations of chaos shook, that they might fall down upon those who are in chaos and might destroy them. And again I ran up to my root of light, lest they be destroyed before the time.

"Still for a third time I went – I am the light which exists in the light, I am the remembrance of the Pronoia – that I might enter into the midst of darkness and the inside of Hades. And I filled my face with the light of the completion of their aeon. And I entered into the midst of their prison, which is the prison of the body. And I said, 'He who hears, let him get up from the deep sleep.' And he wept and shed tears. Bitter tears he wiped from himself and he said, 'Who is it that calls my name, and from where has this hope come to me, while I am in the chains of the prison?' And I said, 'I am the Pronoia of the pure light; I am the thinking of the virginal Spirit, who raised you up to the honored place. Arise and remember that it is you who hearkened, and follow your root, which is I, the merciful one, and guard yourself against the angels of poverty and the demons of chaos and all those who ensnare you, and beware of the deep sleep and the enclosure of the inside of Hades.

"And I raised him up, and sealed him in the light of the water with five seals, in order that death might not have power over him from this time on.

"And behold, now I shall go up to the perfect aeon. I have completed everything for you in your hearing. And I have said everything to you that you might write them down and give them secretly to your fellow spirits, for this is the mystery of the immovable race."

And the savior presented these things to him that he might write them down and keep them secure. And he said to him, "Cursed be everyone who will exchange these things for a gift or for food or for drink or for clothing or for any other such thing." And these things were presented to him in a mystery, and immediately he disappeared from him. And he went to his fellow disciples and related to them what the savior had told him.

Jesus Christ, Amen.

The Apocryphon According to John

A commentary to *The Apocryphon of John*

U p to now our narration was exactly following the text of *The Secret Doctrine*. The reader might have noticed that everything that was presented was just a set of quotations linked with each other by a general subject of Good and Evil and the subjects of separate chapters. Now for the first time we will break away from the customary ground of *The Secret Doctrine*, just because *The Apocryphon of John* as such is not expounded there. Let's try to focus our attention on certain points in this text, following the Spirit of *The Secret Doctrine*.

So, John, a disciple of Jesus, sincerely decided to clarify for himself certain questions connected with the Teaching of Christ, which the Heaven did with a good grace. "The Heaven opened", and he saw a young man who became like an old man and then again changed his appearance and became like a child. It was "the undefiled and incorruptible one", who is near us all the time.

Further on He speaks about Himself – that it was He who "appeared in the form of an eagle on the tree of knowledge, which is the Epinoia from the foreknowledge of the pure light". If we resort to the usual terminology, we can identify this Being with the Higher Logos, the manifestation of which is invisibly present in our Christ-Selves.

And further on this Being states very succinctly the progression of all the events from the moment of creation of this universe – in fact, a summary of the Bible. But the interpretation of the events looks entirely different. And it stands to reason why this apocryphon was safely eliminated by the Church fathers and many others similar to it were destroyed. Why should the flock know the Truth? Any church rests on three pillars: dogma, the leadership mania of the church hierarchy and the ignorance of the masses. *The Secret Doctrine,* in the form in which it was published by Blavatsky and in the form in which it was given by all the Initiated in all times including Jesus' time, destroys the dogma on which the church is based. And as to people's leadership mania and ignorance – people should part with those themselves.

People do everything to save and keep their imperfections. How could one manage to so craftily alter beyond recognition the Teaching given by Jesus, to muddle together Light and Darkness and to combine the uncombinable. After all, the Christian church contrived to combine the Teaching of Jesus with the pharisaic teaching of Jehovah. And during two thousand years the Christians of the whole world have been practising this teaching which has led them knee-deep in blood. What price Crusades, inquisition, burning of the undesirable on bonfires under the pretence of the fight with the servants of the devil? And the myth about the personal Devil, Satan, Lucifer, with whom it is necessary to fight, is the very pillar on which the Christian church is based.

Yet all this is going on. Only the methods have changed. Nowadays the undesirable are declared to be mad, they are killed, imprisoned or just disappear without a trace. This is more civilised for sure.

But let us return to the subject of Good and Evil. In *The Apocryphon of John* in the paragraphs from 4 to 9 it is told about how the higher spheres and the Divine prototype of man were created. But once the first differentiation in the space occurred and the Thought – Epinoia – appeared, this already initiated the beginning of the duality in the universe. The thought is prone to experimentation; it is imperceptible, self-willed and crafty. Sooner or later the time came when it wished, through ignorance, to generate its own creation without the sanction of the Higher Will. However I, for instance, do not have complete confidence that the creation of the material universe was outside the plans of the Creator. What else could substitute that gigantic stage for the souls, on which they can play their roles, develop, passing through suffering and pain, perfecting themselves and achieving the highest state they are capable of?

So, the Thought created Ilda Baoth (Yaltabaoth). *The Secret Doctrine* identifies him with the Sefira of Bina or with Jehovah.

Certainly, the speech is about the things that are beyond our understanding, and that is why everything in the apocryphon is explained in simple words. But any simplification is always fraught with pitfalls. Therefore, my biggest fear is that this Jehovah might take the place of Lucifer in our human consciousness. It is not all as easy as it sounds. Due to the great density of the veil separating our physical world from the higher spheres it sometimes happens that a prophet, a clairvoyant, hears what he wants to hear, but not what is said. It should not be forgotten that John lived 2000 years ago, but Gods "had departed" in the times of the Third Root Race. It is true that later there were Divine Dynasties in the times of the Fourth Root Race, but still distinct clairvoyance and clairaudience were innate abilities of humanity at least a few hundreds thousand years ago. Probably, John overhumanified the Elohim, including Jehovah. And the root of his disfavour of this category of the Divinities lies in the aspiration to lay down a new religion, a more progressive one. But the old one, naturally, must be destroyed. Our religious systems and convictions conform to the level of our consciousness. It is impossible for a perfect religious system or a perfect Teaching to appear under restrictions of an imperfect consciousness. It will be simply neither understood nor accepted by anyone. That is why Gods cannot incarnate in our times. Nobody will take them seriously. Our level of consciousness and our vibrations measure up to those religious systems which we have. Something that is more perfect escapes our notice. We do not understand what the speech is about. An example is *The Secret Doctrine* given through Blavatsky which represents an explanation of a worldview system that was known to humanity from the early days and left all the modern religions far behind. Who of the readers is capable of understanding at least 20 per cent of the subject matter of all the three volumes of *The Secret Doctrine*? This book was given for many centuries ahead. Perhaps, exactly for this purpose the Masters of Wisdom from Shambala El Morya and Kuthumi undertook incarnation.

Later related Teachings appeared, the most well-known of which are Agni Yoga, the Movement I AM, the Bridge of Freedom and the Summit Lighthouse. The founders of these Teachings give the same Truth, but much more simply. This measures up to the level of consciousness of a much greater number of people and finds followers all around the world.

A similar process took place after the death of Jesus when attempts to conform the Teaching given by Him to the understanding of the masses were undertaken. Eventually, from there Christianity ensued that we have nowadays and that contains very little from the true Teaching of Christ, but is comprehensible for millions.

I would like to mention one more point. For some reason new teachings or religions prefer to absorb into themselves inclusions of the old teachings. This happened with the Teaching of Jesus as well when, after the full confirmation of a new religion – Christianity – it appeared to be including both the Old and the New Testaments with all their contradictions and bewilderments. It is interesting to mention that the Teaching of the Ascended Masters given through the Prophets, apart from the new, for the Western consciousness, notions about reincarnation and karma, preferred to absorb as one of its radicals the dogma of Western Christianity about Lucifer and the fallen angels.

Along with a beautiful teaching on the Guardian of the Threshold, on the Cosmic Clock, the main enemy still remains Lucifer, the Devil, who dwells somewhere outside humanity, is the main enemy of humanity and is to be fought with. The Masters cannot give through their Messenger any information which the external consciousness of the Messenger does not accept. That is why the Masters had to annunciate the second death of Lucifer and Satan[168]. However, up to now the followers of this Teaching keep on fighting with the fallen angels. The task of God is to separate the wheat from the chaff among the human monads. Our task is to separate the wheat from the chaff within ourselves.

Let us return to *The Apocryphon of John*. Well, Jehovah, Ilda Baoth, proclaimed: "I AM God, and there is no other God but me."

And he fathered his creation which had an imperfection. And the mother of Ilda Baoth – Epinoia – understood that she had made a mistake, and repented. She was displaced to the ninth heaven until she would

---

[168] In the glossary of Saint Germain's book *Studies in Alchemy* it is written that Lucifer went through the second death on April 26, 1975 and Satan went through the second death on January 27, 1982.

correct her imperfection. How should the correction of this imperfection be done?

A moment came when Ilda Baoth decided to create man "in God's image and his own likeness". This is described in detail in the apocryphon. However, the creation that Ilda Baoth made was not successful. "Their work was incomplete and immobile for a long time." A Being from the higher spheres had to intervene in order for man to come alive.

"And he sent, through his beneficent Spirit and his great mercy, a helper to Adam, luminous Epinoia which comes out of him, who is called Life. And she assists the whole creature, by toiling with him and by restoring him to his fullness and by teaching him about the descent of his seed (and) by teaching him about the way of ascent, (which is) the way he came down. And the luminous Epinoia was hidden in Adam, in order that the archons might not know her, but that the Epinoia might be a correction of the deficiency of the mother.

"And the man came forth because of the shadow of the light which is in him. And his thinking was superior to all those who had made him. When they looked up, they saw that his thinking was superior."

In other words, man obtained his Reason, his Logos, his Saviour that enables him to dare and to achieve the summits of the Divine Perfection.

And here the "Creators" became jealous, when they saw that man was much more elevated than they. And further on there is the scene of the banishment from paradise.

The Secret Doctrine makes it possible to understand the further narration about the birth of Cain, Abel and Seth.

"This will show the esoteric point. The sexless Race was their first production, a modification of and

from themselves, the pure spiritual existences; and this was Adam solus. Thence came the second Race: Adam-Eve or Jod-Heva, inactive androgynes; and finally the Third, or the 'Separating Hermaphrodite', Cain and Abel, who produce the Fourth, Seth-Enos, etc. It is that Third, the last semi-spiritual race, which was also the last vehicle of the divine and innate Wisdom, ingenerate in the Enochs, the Seers of that Mankind. The Fourth, which had tasted from the fruit of the Tree of Good and Evil – Wisdom united already to earthy, and therefore impure, intelligence had consequently to acquire that Wisdom by initiation and great struggle."[169]

"The verses in Genesis from chs. i. to v., are purposely mixed up for Kabalistic reasons. After MAN of Genesis ch. i. 26 and Enos, Son of Man of ch. iv. v. 26, after Adam, the first androgyne, after Adam Kadmon, the sexless (the first) Logos, Adam and Eve once separated, come finally Jehovah-Eve[170] and Cain-Jehovah[171]. These represent distinct Root-Races, for millions of years elapsed between them."[172]

The murder of Abel by Cain indicates nothing but a shedding of the sexual blood, *"...for Habel, the feminine principle, and – child-bearing; a process shown to have begun in the Third Race, or with Adam's THIRD son, Seth, with whose son Henoch, men began to call themselves Jehovah or Jah-hovah, the male Jod and Havah or Eve – to wit, male and female beings."[173]*

---

[169] The Secret Doctrine, Vol. 2, p. 134
[170] Abel.
[171] Cain.
[172] The Secret Doctrine, Vol. 2, p. 127
[173] *Ibid.*, p. 469

"...the first and original meaning of Enos, the son of Seth, was the First Race born in the present usual way from man and woman – for Seth is no man, but a race. Before him humanity was hermaphrodite. While Seth is the first result (physiologically) after the FALL, he is also the first man; hence his son Enos is referred to as the 'Son of man'. Seth represents the later Third Race."[174]

Jehovah also represents the forefathers of the human race, Pitri, who came from the Moon. That is why he is a Moon Spirit who became an Earthly Spirit.

"It is only in his capacity of the genius of the moon, the latter being credited in the old cosmogony with being the parent of our Earth, that Jehovah could ever be regarded as the creator of our globe and its Heaven, namely, the Firmament."[175]

I read the next passage from the apocryphon very attentively:

"...he[176] (the chief archon) had brought darkness upon the whole earth.

"And he made a plan with his powers. He sent his angels to the daughters of men, that they might take some of them for themselves and raise offspring for their enjoyment. And at first they did not succeed. When they had no success, they gathered together again and they made a plan together. They created a counterfeit spirit, who resembles the Spirit who had descended, so as to pollute the souls through it. And the angels changed themselves in their likeness into the likeness of their mates (the daughters of men), filling them with the spirit of darkness, which they had mixed

---

[174] The Secret Doctrine, Vol. 2, p. 125-126
[175] *Ibid.*, p. 474
[176] Ilda Baoth or Jehovah

for them, and with evil. They brought gold and silver and a gift and copper and iron and metal and all kinds of things. And they steered the people who had followed them into great troubles, by leading them astray with many deceptions. They (the people) became old without having enjoyment. They died, not having found truth and without knowing the God of truth. And thus the whole creation became enslaved forever, from the foundation of the world until now. And they took women and begot children out of the darkness according to the likeness of their spirit. And they closed their hearts, and they hardened themselves through the hardness of the counterfeit spirit until now."

Is this the description of the true fall of angels? *The Secret Doctrine* says nothing about it. In fact it actually passes over any points capable of generating a wish to fight with anybody. The only phrase from *The Secret Doctrine* with which I can associate this passage from the apocryphon sounds thus:

"It (mankind) became divided. Two-thirds of it were ruled by Dynasties of lower, material Spirits of the earth, who took possession of the easily accessible bodies; one-third remained faithful, and joined with the nascent Fifth Race – the divine Incarnates."[177]

I think that both passages do not say that the "fallen angels" seized the temples of men. They say that the majority of people did biddings of their lower nature – the moon, astral part of their lower Self, which completely deprives us of the contact with the Divine part of ourselves. We voluntarily choose the illusion of this world, fall into error and gloominess and get into the clutches of those forces that swirl a soul until it awakens from its lethargy. The two thirds of humanity

---

[177] The Secret Doctrine, Vol. 2, p. 350

have enough millions of years ahead in order to know the Truth. And those who are resistant gradually turn into the retarded evolutions similar to the Australian aborigines and disappear from the face of the Earth. God and Nature have enough ways to correct our evolution and to exhort us in our fight with our lower Ego, or the Guardian of the Threshold – according to the terminology of the Teaching of the Ascended Masters.

"For it is this Ego, with its fierce Selfishness and animal desire to live a Senseless life (Tanha), which is 'the maker of the tabernacle,' as Buddha calls it in Dhammapada (153 and 154). Hence the expression, 'the Spirits of the Earth clothed the shadows and expanded them'. To these 'Spirits' belong temporarily the human astral selves; and it is they who give, or build, the physical tabernacle of man, for the Monad and its conscious principle, Manas...

"... In sober truth, vice and wickedness are an abnormal, unnatural manifestation, at this period of our human evolution – at least they ought to be so. The fact that mankind was never more selfish and vicious than it is now, civilized nations having succeeded in making of the first an ethical characteristic, of the second an art, is an additional proof of the exceptional nature of the phenomenon."[178]

I consciously explain this moment with the two thirds of humanity to avert someone from a desire to start fighting with these two thirds. Yet, history knows lots of examples when the most absurd conclusions were made by ignorant heads even from fairly right

---

[178] The Secret Doctrine, Vol. 2, p. 110

theories. Only a short time ago the full-blooded Arians in the fight for the purity of the Arian race annihilated several tens of millions people. And this happened within the memory of the living men!

The Apocryphon of John is written in quite simple language and I am leaving its further observation to the intuition of the readers.

I will also take the liberty to give my personal understanding of how the elimination of the imperfection of our universe will take place. Man has obtained Reason, Consciousness, Christ Self. And this is the force that he must discover in himself under the coverings of the material body. Once man finds God within himself and establishes connection with Him, man will alter his consciousness. By the example of Australia that still has practically unchanged species of flora and fauna due to the fact that its population was composed for a long time by the retarded evolutions of the Third Root Race, we see that the entire world around us depends on and changes in accordance with the changing of our consciousness. The nearer our consciousness is to the Divine pattern, the more subtle forms the physical world takes. In this way the physical universe gradually contracts, becomes more spiritual and, finally, returns to its source, the Creator. The cycle of the Universe will come to an end. In how many eons of years will it happen? Only God knows. But it will take place with our help, with the help of man, through the changing of our consciousness.

Many meanings of the battle in heaven

Since the views of modern man regarding the "battle in heaven" are mainly based on *The Revelation* of John the Beloved, let us recall what is said there about this battle.

A great and wondrous sign appeared in heaven: a woman clothed with the sun, with the moon under her feet and a crown of twelve stars on her head. She was pregnant and cried out in pain as she was about to give birth. Then another sign appeared in heaven: an enormous red dragon with seven heads and ten horns and seven crowns on his heads. His tail swept a third of the stars out of the sky and flung them to the earth. The dragon stood in front of the woman who was about to give birth, so that he might devour her child the moment it was born. She gave birth to a son, a male child, who will rule all the nations with an iron scepter. And her child was snatched up to God and to his throne. The woman fled into the desert to a place prepared for her by God, where she might be taken care of for 1,260 days.

And there was war in heaven. Michael and his angels fought against the dragon, and the dragon and his angels fought back. But he was not strong enough, and they lost their place in heaven. The great dragon was hurled down – that ancient serpent called the devil, or Satan, who leads the whole world astray. He was hurled to the earth, and his angels with him. [179]

---

[179] Rev. 12:1-9.

It is known how this passage is interpreted by Christianity. On the whole, exactly the same interpretation is given to it by the Teaching of the Ascended Masters. The fallen angels who did not keep their dignity were cast from the higher spheres down to the Earth. And all the problems of humanity are connected with these fallen who have infiltrated to all the spheres of our life. It would be interesting to know how this very passage is interpreted by *The Secret Doctrine* and whether it is possible to interpret it somehow differently.

To begin with, it should be mentioned that *The Revelation* of John the Beloved *(The Apocalypse)* is not the only known source telling about the battle in heaven. In practically all the religions Gods are constantly fighting among themselves. What price the great battle between the Gods and the Asuras in Mahabharata?

In ancient Babylon Bel confronts the Dragon. In ancient Greece Apollo kills Python. Krishna kills the five-headed Kalia. In ancient Egypt Typhon hacks Osiris into fourteen parts and then Horus kills Typhon, or Anopis, the Dragon.

In order to understand the core of these battles one should know the ancient religions of these countries inside out. But one thing is certain: all the religions reflect some general events which are proficiently camouflaged under allegory.

We have *The Secret Doctrine* at our disposal, and let us try to find together how the "battle in heaven" is interpreted in it.

Let us begin with the symbol of the serpent or dragon. Due to *The Apocalypse* we used to equate the serpent and the dragon with the Evil. The fallen angels are called serpents, and the dragon is associated with the Devil himself.

However, it was not always so. *"...the Dragon was never regarded as Evil, nor was the Serpent either – in antiquity. In the metaphors, whether astronomical, cosmical, theogonical or simply physiological, i.e., phallic – the Serpent was always regarded as a divine symbol."* [180]

"The serpent has ever been the symbol of the adept, and of his powers of immortality and divine knowledge...

"Every people of antiquity reverenced this symbol, with the exception of Christians, who chose to forget the brazen Serpent of Moses [181], *and even the implied acknowledgment of the great wisdom and prudence of the Serpent by Jesus himself, 'Be ye wise as serpents and harmless as doves."* [182]

"The Angels fallen into generation are referred to metaphorically as Serpents and Dragons of Wisdom.

...

"Thus the remark [183] *made by the great Initiate (in Luke x. 18) – one that referred allegorically to the ray*

---

[180] The Secret Doctrine, Vol. 2, p. 505

[181] See *Numbers* xxi. 8-9. God orders Moses to build a brazen Serpent "Saraph"; *to look upon which* heals those bitten by the *fiery serpents*.

[182] The Secret Doctrine, Vol. 2, p. 364

[183] To make it plainer, any one who reads that passage in *Luke,* will see that the remark follows the report of the *seventy,* who rejoice that "even the devils (the spirit of controversy and reasoning, or the opposing power, since Satan means simply "*adversary*" or *opponent*) are subject unto us through thy name." (*Luke* x. 17.) Now, "thy name" means the name of Christos, or Logos, or the spirit of true divine wisdom, as distinct from the spirit of intellectual or mere materialistic reasoning – the HIGHER SELF in short. And when Jesus remarks to this that he has "beheld Satan as lightning fall from heaven," it is a mere statement of his clairvoyant powers, notifying them that he already knew it, and a reference to the incarnation of the divine ray (the gods or angels) which *falls into generation.* For not all men, by any means, benefit by that incarnation, and with some the power remains latent and dead during the whole life. Truly

of Enlightenment and reason, falling like lightning from on high into the hearts and minds of the converts to that old wisdom-religion then presented in a new form by the wise Galilean Adept – was distorted out of recognition (as was his own personality), and made to fit in with one of the most cruel as the most pernicious of all theological dogmas."[184]

Therefore, when Jesus said, "I saw Satan falling like lightning from heaven"[185], *"this remark refers to divine Wisdom falling like lightning on, and quickening the intellects of those who fight the devils of ignorance and superstition"[186].*

If we turn to the Teaching of the Ascended Masters that has to use some ancient symbols, we will discover, to our surprise, now the focus of Serapis Bey twined with snakes, then Guan Yin entering the space of this Teaching on a Dragon.

"The hierophants, moreover, of Egypt, as of Babylon, generally styled themselves the

---

"No man knoweth who the Son is, but the Father; and who the Father is, but the Son" as added by Jesus then and there (*Ibid* v. 22) — the Church "of Christ" less than any one else. The Initiates alone understood the secret meaning of the term "Father and the Son," and knew that it referred to Spirit and Soul on the Earth. For the teachings of Christ were *occult* teachings, which could only be explained *at the initiation.* They were never intended for the masses, for Jesus forbade the twelve to go to the Gentiles and the Samaritans (*Matt.* x. 8), and repeated to his disciples that the "mysteries of Heaven" were for them alone, not for the multitudes (*Mark* iv. 11). (The footnote is copied from the book *The Secret Doctrine*, p. 231)

[184] The Secret Doctrine, Vol. 2, p. 230-231
[185] Luke 10:18.
[186] The Secret Doctrine, Vol. 2, p. 230

*'Sons of the Serpent-god', or 'Sons of the Dragon',
during the mysteries.*"[187]

And while the symbol of the serpent was sometimes
applicable to the adepts of the left hand, *"...as a
Dragon it had never been anything else than a symbol
of the manifested Deity in its great Wisdom."*[188]

*"This 'Dragon' having a septenary meaning, the
highest and the lowest may be given. The former is
identical with the 'Self-born', the Logos (the Hindu
Aja). He was the second person of the Trinity, the
SON, with the Christian Gnostics called the
Naasenians, or Serpent-Worshippers. His symbol was
the constellation of the Dragon.*[189] *Its seven 'stars' are
the seven stars held in the hand of the 'Alpha and
Omega' in Revelation. In its most terrestrial meaning,
the term 'Dragon' was applied to the Wise men.*
*"This portion of the religious symbolism of
antiquity is very abstruse and mysterious, and may
remain incomprehensible to the profane. In our
modern day it so jars on the Christian ear that it can
hardly escape, all civilization notwithstanding, being
regarded as a direct denunciation of the most
cherished Christian dogmas..."*[190]

The fact that the ancients treated serpents and
especially dragons decently makes us think about why
Archangel Michael still does kill this Dragon. And if

---

[187] The Secret Doctrine, Vol. 2, p. 379
[188] *Ibid.*, p. 387
[189] As shown by H. Lizeray in the "Trinite Chretienne Devoilee" – placed
between the immutable Father (the Pole, a fixed Point) and mutable
matter, the Dragon transmits to the latter the influences received by him
from the Pole, whence his name – the *Verbum*.
[190] The Secret Doctrine, Vol. 2, p. 355

we remember that *The Secret Doctrine* writes about Michael as a surrogate of Jehovah *("...Michael being simply Jehovah himself, one of the subordinate Spirits at best."[191])*, then the sense fades away altogether. In that case what interpretation of the "battle in heaven" does *The Secret Doctrine* offer?

Let us remember that each event and every symbol can be read with the help of seven keys. Let us try to find some of these keys in *The Secret Doctrine*. First of all it should be noted that the speech is about three different wars.

"The first war happened in the night of time, between the gods the (A)-suras, and lasted for the period of one 'divine year'[192]."[193]

Let us remember that at first the universe expands and is created with the help of the Cosmic Forces and after that it contracts. Therefore, *"...the 'woman with child' of Revelation (xii.) was Aime, the great mother, or Binah, the third Sephiroth, 'whose name is Jehovah'; and the 'Dragon,' who seeks to devour her coming child (the Universe), is the Dragon of absolute Wisdom – that Wisdom which, recognising the non-separateness of the Universe and everything in it from the Absolute ALL, sees in it no better than the great Illusion, Mahamaya, hence the cause of misery and suffering."[194]*

---

[191] *Ibid.*, p. 508

[192] One "Day of Brahmâ" lasting 4,320,000,000 years – multiply this by 365! The Asuras here (no-gods, but demons) are still *Suras*, gods higher in hierarchy than such secondary gods as are not even mentioned in the Vedas. The duration of the war shows its significance, and that they are only the personified Cosmic powers.

[193] The Secret Doctrine, **Vol. 1**, p. 419

[194] The Secret Doctrine, Vol. 2, p. 384, footnote.

Another war took place on the Earth during the "creation of man". Let us remember again that at first the Masters of Wisdom refused to create, though the time to create had come. This can be considered as enmity with the Law and with those Elohim who followed the Law. And what the Masters of Wisdom are doing constantly while residing on Earth, regardless of where it is – in Shambala or as "a part of a part"[195] in our Christ Selves – they are awaking our consciousness and through this awakening they force our consciousness to change. And through the change of our consciousness this world changes too, gradually becoming more subtle and returning to the One. And again, they enter a battle with those forces that defend materiality. That is why when Archangel Michael slays the Dragon, this can be considered as casting the Masters of Wisdom down from the heavenly spheres into the matter for many cycles of embodiments within people's bodies.

If we look at this event with another key, it can be considered as a triumph of the external exoteric religions, based on dogma and cult, over the Secret Wisdom.

"The 'Fall' is a universal allegory. It sets forth at one end of the ladder of Evolution the 'rebellion,' i.e., the action of differentiating intellection or consciousness on its various planes, seeking union with matter; and at the other, the lower end, the rebellion of matter against Spirit, or of action against spiritual inertia. And here lies the germ of an error which has had such disastrous effects on the intelligence of civilized societies for over 1,800 years.

---

[195] For the explanation of this term "a part of a part" see *The Secret Doctrine*, Vol. 2, p. 359.

In the original allegory it is matter – hence the more material angels – which was regarded as the conqueror of Spirit, or the Archangels who 'fell' on this plane. 'They of the flaming sword (or animal passions) had put to flight the Spirits of Darkness.' Yet it is the latter who fought for the supremacy of the conscious and divine spirituality on Earth and failed, succumbing to the power of matter. But in theological dogma we see the reverse. It is Michael, 'who is like unto God,' the representative of Jehovah, who is the leader of the celestial hosts... who has the best of Satan. It is true that the nature of Michael depends upon that of his Creator and Master."[196]

"Strange to say, the Occult teaching reverses the characters; it is the anthropomorphous archangel with the Christians, and the man-like God with the Hindus, which represent matter in this case; and the Dragon, or Serpent, Spirit. Occult symbolism furnishes the key to the mystery; theological symbolics conceal it still more. For the former explains many a saying in the Bible and even in the New Testament which have hitherto remained incomprehensible; while the latter, owing to its dogma of Satan and his rebellion, has belittled the character and nature of its would-be infinite, absolutely perfect god, and created the greatest evil and curse on earth – belief in a personal Devil. This mystery is opened with the key to its metaphysical symbolism now restored; while that of theological interpretation shows the gods and the archangels standing as symbols for the dead letter or dogmatic religions, and as arrayed against the pure truths of Spirit, naked and unadorned with fancy.

---

[196] The Secret Doctrine, Vol. 2, p. 62

"Many were the hints thrown out in this direction in 'Isis Unveiled,' and a still greater number of references to this mystery may be found scattered throughout these volumes. To make the point clear once for all: that which the clergy of every dogmatic religion – pre-eminently the Christian – points out as Satan, the enemy of God, is in reality, the highest divine Spirit – (occult Wisdom on Earth) – in its naturally antagonistic character to every worldly, evanescent illusion, dogmatic or ecclesiastical religions included."[197]

"The Third Race was pre-eminently the bright shadow, at first, of the gods, whom tradition exiles on Earth after the allegorical war in Heaven; which became still more allegorical on Earth, for it was the war between spirit and matter. This war will last till the inner and divine man adjusts his outer terrestrial self to his own spiritual nature. Till then the dark and fierce passions of the former will be at eternal feud with his master, the Divine Man. But the animal will be tamed one day, because its nature will be changed, and harmony will reign once more between the two as before the 'Fall,' when even mortal man was created by the Elements and was not born."[198]

The third war is mentioned as one that took place at the end of the Fourth Race between its Adepts and the Adepts of the Fifth Race, i.e. between the Initiated of "The Sacred Island" and the wizards of the Atlantis.

And this last war is going on, in my view, to the present day. This is the war between the representatives of the Spirit, the Initiated, and the representatives of

---

[197] The Secret Doctrine, Vol. 2, p. 377
[198] *Ibid.*, p. 268

any Church. And it always ends in a visible victory of the representatives of the official religion. Visible in this earthly plane. But in the spiritual plane the Initiated always win the battle. It is enough to recall the example of Jesus. John the Baptist noted that during his crucifixion Jesus was also pierced with a spear ("one of the soldiers pierced Jesus' side with a spear"[199]). And he wrote about it, who knows, maybe for a bigger likeness with the scene of Archangel Michael's slaying the Dragon. The Dragons of Wisdom do not fight. They affirm the Truth and always win! Because the death of the physical body does not matter at all.

Victimhood, self-sacrifice, unselfishness are those characteristics that help distinguish the true service from its look-alike – a false, hypocritical, ostentatious service to dogma or false gods who have taken the place of the One, the Unknowable, the Absolute.

"Furthermore, the 'War in Heaven' is shown, in one of its significations, to have meant and referred to those terrible struggles in store for the candidate for adeptship, between himself and his (by magic) personified human passions, when the inner enlightened man had to either slay them or fail. In the former case he became the 'Dragon-Slayer,' as having happily overcome all the temptations; and a 'Son of the Serpent' and a Serpent himself, having cast off his old skin and being born in a new body, becoming a Son of Wisdom and Immortality in Eternity."[200]

Returning to *The Revelation* again, I will give a passage from *The Secret Doctrine* which will help in the interpretation of some points of this document.

---

[199] John 19:34.
[200] The Secret Doctrine, Vol. 2, p. 380

"Whatever interpretation profane mystics may give to the famous Chapter xvii., with its riddle of the woman in purple and scarlet; whether Protestants nod at the Roman Catholics, when reading 'MYSTERY, BABYLON THE GREAT, THE MOTHER OF HARLOTS AND ABOMINATIONS OF THE EARTH,' or Roman Catholics glare at the Protestants, the Occultists pronounce, in their impartiality, that these words have applied from the first to all and every exoteric Churchianity, that which was the 'ceremonial magic' of old, with its terrible effects, and is now the harmless (because distorted) farce of ritualistic worship. The 'mystery' of the woman and of the beast, are the symbols of soul-killing Churchianity and of SUPERSTITION. 'The beast that was, and is not, and yet is.' 'And here is the Mind which hath wisdom. The seven heads are seven mountains (seven continents and seven races) on which the woman sitteth,' the symbol of all the exoteric, barbarous, idolatrous faiths which have covered that symbol 'with the blood of the saints and the blood of the martyrs' who protested and do protest. 'And there are seven Kings (seven races); five are fallen (our fifth race included), and one is (the fifth continues), and the other (the sixth and the seventh races) is not yet come... And when he (the race 'King') cometh, he must continue a short space' (v. 10). There are many such Apocalyptic allusions, but the student has to find them out for himself."[201]

---

[201] The Secret Doctrine, Vol. 2, p. 748

A comparative analysis of some statements of *The Secret Doctrine* by Blavatsky and the Teaching of the Ascended Masters given through the Prophets

E ven a sketchy knowledge of the Teaching of the Ascended Masters given through Mark and Elizabeth Prophet and a similar sketchy knowledge of *The Secret Doctrine,* at least within the scope given in this publication, is enough to see certain discrepancies in these two Teachings. In fact, there are two basic discrepancies and they are: the Teaching on Ascension and the Teaching on the fallen angels.

Let us try to analyse these discrepancies. In the Teaching of the Ascended Masters the concept of Ascension is described in detail. This is a state which can be achieved by following the path of the Teaching of the Ascended Masters. In the glossary of Saint Germain's book *Studies in Alchemy: The Science of Self-Transformation,* one can find a definition of Ascension:

> *"The ritual whereby the soul reunites with the Spirit of the Living God, the I AM Presence. The ascension is the culmination of the soul's God-victorious sojourn in time and space. It is the reward of the righteous that is the gift of God after the last judgment before the great white throne in which every man is judged 'according to their works'."*

In order to achieve Ascension man must transmute no less than 51 percent of karma, balance the threefold flame and fulfill his Divine plan. Besides, it is said in the Teaching that the first two human Races ascended after they had passed through seven male and seven female incarnations. But in the times of the Third Race, due to the rebellion of angels and their fall to the Earth and after they had tempted people with the amenities of earthly life, people got entrapped on this planet for many hundreds and thousands of incarnations. But, through using the Teachings on karma and on the Guardian of the Threshold, through keeping straight and transmuting the personal and the planet's karma and through reading the decrees of the violet flame, everyone can achieve Ascension already upon completion of the current life-span.

In truth, I do not see major discrepancies between this Teaching on Ascension and the statements of *The Secret Doctrine*. Perhaps, the only downside is a certain simplification of the evolution of the Races done by the Prophets. However, if we take into consideration that the Teaching of the Ascended Masters was given by the Prophets in a Christian country amidst the people brought up on the Christian dogmas, when everybody was sure that God created a new soul before the birth of each man, the understanding of the duration of the path of a soul through many incarnations was a great progress. And the aim itself – the Ascension – sensitised people to aspire for more elevated states of consciousness than merely living on earth in the physical body.

The Secret Doctrine just discloses the frames of the evolutionary path to a still greater degree. And for many people such a perspective of the soul's wandering through the seven Races on each of the seven globes and not on just one planet seems, perhaps, wearisome and evoking despair and boredom.

That is why the Truth can be divulged only according to the level of consciousness and, perhaps, obtaining of the entire truth at once can even be pernicious. It is akin to an attempt to squeeze into a pot more than it can contain. The pot, finally, may not withstand the overload and crack. That is why the self-preservation instinct sometimes makes people physically destroy the source of the Truth which, in their opinion, hinders their quiet life.

The Teaching on Ascension can also be applied to the scheme of evolution of the Races given in *The Secret Doctrine*. Just this Ascension is postponed for a few billion or trillion years till the end of this universe.

However, it is possible to speak about an intermediate ascension after each Race. The Human Races in this case can be compared with the grades at school. And each incarnation can be identified with a school week or day. Among the students there are individuals with different abilities. There are A-students and there are underachievers. For some it is enough to study in one grade for one year, some repeat the year, and some people have to repeat the year for the third time. There are also those who can complete one or two grades ahead of schedule, quickly achieving the level of consciousness necessary for the graduation class. But there is also a college or a university ahead.

If we apply this to the human Races, there are individuals who have already achieved the level of consciousness of the Sixth Race, while at present the Fourth and the Fifth Races are still incarnating. But these individuals cannot incarnate before the cosmic due time. So they are awaiting this time in the subtle plane. But these souls are A-students who have left all the others behind, so once they start their succession of incarnations, for those peoples and in those countries where they will start to incarnate and will comprise the bulk of the population, the Golden Age will come. At the same time the rest of humanity who remain in the

Fifth Race will still stay in the Kali Yuga for more than 400 thousand years until the fifth and the sixth sub-races of the Fifth Root Race stop incarnating.

As regards the doctrine on the fallen angels, the situation here is not as optimistic. For what happens, as a matter of fact? On their altars people keep the focuses of the Ascended Masters and worship them.

Who are the Ascended Masters? They are Higher Beings who reside in the higher plane, including Shambala, and teach humanity. *The Secret Doctrine* teaches that the Masters of Wisdom reside in Shambala and have been teaching humanity during millions of years since the time of the second half of the Third Root Race, since the moment of the so-called fall of humanity. And among them there are Jesus, Gautama Buddha, Kuthumi, El Morya and others.

From *The Secret Doctrine* we know that at first these Masters of Wisdom were residing among the people of the Third Race and directly teaching them. Then the "Gods departed" in order to come again as Divine Dynasties in the times of the Fourth Root Race, and after that they incarnated as Heroes during the third sub-race of the Fifth Root Race. And many of them sacrificed themselves and undertook partial incarnations in our time. I will give a passage from *The Secret Doctrine* from where the above-mentioned follows.

"When mortals shall have become sufficiently spiritualised, there will be no more need of forcing them into a correct comprehension of ancient Wisdom. Men will know then, that there never yet was a great World-reformer, whose name has passed into our generation, who (a) was not a direct emanation of the LOGOS (under whatever name known to us), i.e., an essential incarnation of one of 'the seven,' of the

'divine Spirit who is sevenfold'; and (b) who had not appeared before, during the past Cycles. They will recognise, then, the cause which produces in history and chronology certain riddles of the ages; the reason why, for instance, it is impossible for them to assign any reliable date to Zoroaster, who is found multiplied by twelve and fourteen in the Dabistan; why the Rishis and Manus are so mixed up in their numbers and individualities; why Krishna and Buddha speak of themselves as re-incarnations, i.e., Krishna is identified with the Rishi Narayana, and Gautama gives a series of his previous births; and why the former, especially, being 'the very supreme Brahma,' is yet called Amsamsavatara – 'a part of a part' only of the Supreme on Earth. Finally, why Osiris is a great God, and at the same time a 'prince on Earth,' who reappears in Thoth-Hermes, and why Jesus (in Hebrew, Joshua) of Nazareth is recognised, cabalistically, in Joshua, the Son of Nun, as well as in other personages. The esoteric doctrine explains it by saying that each of these (as many others) had first appeared on earth as one of the seven powers of the LOGOS, individualized as a God or 'Angel' (messenger); then, mixed with matter, they had re-appeared in turn as great sages and instructors who 'taught the Fifth Race,' after having instructed the two preceding races, had ruled during the Divine Dynasties, and had finally sacrificed themselves, to be reborn under various circumstances for the good of mankind, and for its salvation at certain critical periods; until in their last incarnations they had become truly only 'the parts of a part' on earth, though de facto the One Supreme in Nature."[202]

---

[202] The Secret Doctrine, Vol. 2, p. 358-359

Besides, we know from *The Secret Doctrine* that the very same Masters of Wisdom endowed us with our Consciousness, our Reason, our Christ Self and our mental body.

Isn't it obvious that it is impossible to continue keeping these Masters on the altar and worshipping them and simultaneously go on binding them as fallen angels? Isn't it clear that it is impossible to aspire to the connection with one's own Christ Self and to simultaneously fight with it as a fallen angel? Only the dual human consciousness is capable of that.

An analogy between the Teaching of the Ascended Masters and the religion given by the prophet Mohammed – the Mohammedan faith – comes to my mind. I have neither read the Koran nor ever studied Islam. But something in this religion itself leads to an incorrect understanding of the Spiritual War – Jihad. In some way this purely spiritual concept has degenerated into an aspiration for the physical annihilation of the adherents of a different faith: "Kill the disbeliever!" And due to their limited consciousness people prefer to wage this spiritual war with each other in the physical plane. Yet, in fact, there was nothing bad in the wish of the prophet Mohammed to give the basics of Christianity to the peoples of the Central Asia. The slightest implication that the enemy may dwell in someone else, in your neighbour, turns into a disaster with the present miserable level of consciousness of humanity.

Drawing analogies with the Teaching of the Prophets, I also see a sincere wish to give the basics of both the Eastern religions and the esoteric knowledge to the peoples of America and the whole world. But again in the foreground we see a fight, a struggle with the fallen angels who have flooded all the public offices, banks, mass media and religions of the world. A spiritual thought, being a more subtle sphere of the human activities and having taken a wrong direction, is able to engender incorrect actions in all the rest of the spheres of activities. And the war in Iraq, a wish to project the principles of democracy and freedom to the "retarded evolutions" of this country (these are not my words, this is what the Prophets used to teach) by force is, perchance, the first consequence of the incorrectly chosen direction of movement. Maybe the time has come to refocus our minds? Instead of the fight with the mythical fallen angels to try to establish a connection with the "fallen angel" within us, our Christ Self, to help it spread its wings and reunite with its brothers – the Masters of Wisdom in Shambala?

If we take the best horse, a food and water reserve, arm ourselves with the most perfect prayers, mantras and meditations and gallop to the Summit of the Divine Consciousness, we may never reach that summit if we choose to gallop in the wrong direction.

If in each of us there is a spark, a particle of the Ascended Masters in the shape of our Christ Self, isn't it our duty to free this particle, so that the Masters of Wisdom could regain their wholeness and implement their mission on the Earth together with us? It depends on each person that their part of Saint Germain, El Morya, Jesus, Sanat Kumara can ascend. Maybe, this task will seem more elevated and righteous to someone than a total binding and annihilation of the fallen headed by their leader Lucifer? By projecting and duplicating the feeling of combativeness we will reap nothing but a whirlwind. How many thousands or millions of years must pass in order for the human consciousness to become capable of giving up aggression and fighting and together with this to become able to give up any manifestation of Evil and make a conscious choice in favour of the Good?

For this we must loose the fetters of the matter tying our Divine part to the Earth, and slay our Guardian of the Threshold – this true devil.

For those who are in the leadership position of any church, no matter how advanced this church may seem, it makes no difference in front of which decorations they indulge their personal ambitions – whether this be crucified Jesus or the I AM Presence chart. Therefore, everything written here is meant for the genuine Truth seekers, for those whom Jesus addressed: "be wise as serpents and harmless as doves"[203].

If we follow the Path of Jesus Christ and live according to His commandments – is it possible that we have forgotten that Jesus never bound anyone, and even being on the cross He was praying for His torturers: "Father, forgive them, for they don't know what they are doing."[204]?

And this is the Path that all the Initiated followed – a Path of Self-sacrifice, Commitment, Self-denial and Service.

---

[203] Mathew 10:16.
[204] Luke 23:34.

Raphael. Archangel Michael Slaying Satan. 1518

Gustave Moreau. Prometheus. 1868

Prometheus – Lucifer?

*"**T**hat which is part of our souls is eternal',
says Thackeray; and what can be nearer
to our souls than that which happens at the dawns of
our lives? Those lives are countless, but the soul or
spirit that animates us throughout these myriads of
existences is the same; and though 'the book and
volume' of the physical brain may forget events within
the scope of one terrestrial life, the bulk of collective
recollections can never desert the divine soul within
us. Its whispers may be too soft, the sound of its words
too far off the plane perceived by our physical senses;
yet the shadow of events that were, just as much as the
shadow of the events that are to come, is within its
perceptive powers, and is ever present before its
mind's eye.*

*"It is this soul-voice, perhaps, which tells those
who believe in tradition more than in written History,
that what is said below is all true, and relates to pre-
historic facts."[205]*

The legend about Prometheus was committed to
writing and staged in Greece by Aeschylus, who, being
an Initiated, knew very well what he was writing about.
Aeschylus just repeated in drama form what was
revealed to the hierophants during the mysteries. It is
supposed that he was sentenced to stoning to death for
the disclosure of the mystery. Nevertheless, this myth
itself is more ancient than the Hellenes and belongs to
the dawn of human consciousness.

*"The demi-god robs the gods (the Elohim) of their
secret – the mystery of the creative fire. For this
sacrilegious attempt he is struck down by KRONOS[206]*

---

[205] The Secret Doctrine, Vol. 2, p. 424
[206] Kronos is "time," and thus the allegory becomes very suggestive.

and delivered unto Zeus, the FATHER and creator of a mankind which he would wish to have blind intellectually, and animallike; a personal deity, which will not see MAN 'like one of us.' Hence Prometheus, 'the fire and light-giver,' is chained on Mount Caucasus and condemned to suffer torture."[207]

Certainly, the speech in the legend is not about the physical fire. *"For fire was never 'discovered,' but existed on earth since its beginning."[208]*

The speech is about the Creating fire, the fire of Reason that is used in art and creative work, as well as in procreation. The speech is about the fire that was brought to the Earth by the Masters of Wisdom. *"The Crucified Titan is the personified symbol of the collective Logos, the 'Host,' and of the 'Lords of Wisdom' or the HEAVENLY MAN, who incarnated in Humanity."[209]*

"Our Saviours, the Agnishwatta and other divine 'Sons of the Flame of Wisdom' (personified by the Greeks in Prometheus[210], may well, in the injustice of

---

[207] The Secret Doctrine, Vol. 2, p. 414

[208] *Ibid.*, p. 523

[209] *Ibid.*, p. 413

[210] In Mrs. Anna Swanwick's volumes, "The Dramas of Æschylus," it is said of "Prometheus Bound" (Vol. 2, pp. 146, 147), that Prometheus truly appears in it "as the champion and benefactor of mankind, whose condition... is depicted as weak and miserable in the extreme... Zeus, it is said, proposed to annihilate these puny ephemerals, and to plant upon the earth a new race in their stead." We see the Lords of Being doing likewise, and exterminating the first product of nature and the sea, in the Stanzas (V, *et seq.*)... Prometheus *represents* himself as having frustrated this design, and as being consequently subjected, for the sake of mortals, to the most agonising pain, inflicted by the remorseless cruelty of Zeus. We have, thus, the Titan, the symbol of finite reason and free will (of intellectual humanity, or the higher aspect of *Manas*), depicted *as the sublime philanthropist,* while Zeus, the supreme deity of Hellas, is portrayed as the cruel and obdurate despot, a character peculiarly revolting to Athenian sentiment." The reason for it is explained further on. The

the human heart, be left unrecognized and unthanked.
They may, in our ignorance of the truth, be indirectly
cursed for Pandora's gift: but to find themselves
proclaimed and declared by the mouth of the clergy,
the EVIL ONES, is too heavy a Karma for 'Him' 'who
dared alone' – when Zeus 'ardently desired' to quench
the entire human race – to save 'that mortal race'
from perdition.'[211]

If you read footnote 210 attentively, you will see
that there was a pointed question of liquidation of
humanity as an unsuccessful one. Doesn't it remind you
about what is said in the dictation of Sanat Kumara *The
Opening of the Seventh Seal* (see chapter *The Opening
of the Seventh Seal. II The Dispensation Granted*):

"Thus the light of the temples had gone out, and the
purpose to which God had created man – to be the
temple of the living God – was no longer being
fulfilled. One and all were the living dead, a Matter
vessel without an ensouling light, an empty shell.
Nowhere on earth was there a mystery school – not a
chela, not a Guru, no initiates of the path of initiation
unto Christhood.

"The hour of the judgment had come, and the one
seated upon the throne in the center of the twelve times
twelve hierarchies of light had pronounced the word
that was the unanimous consensus of all: Let earth and
her evolutions be rolled up as a scroll and lit as a taper
of the sacred fire. Let all energies misqualified be
returned to the Great Central Sun for repolarization. Let

"Supreme Deity" bears, in every ancient Pantheon – including that of the
Jews – a *dual* character, composed of light and shadow. (The footnote is
copied from the book *The Secret Doctrine*)
[211] The Secret Doctrine, Vol. 2, p. 411

energy misused be realigned and recharged with the light of Alpha and Omega, once again to be infused by the Creator within the ongoing creation of worlds without end.

"The requirement of the law for the saving of Terra? It was that one who should qualify as the embodied Guru, the Lamb, should be present in the physical octave to hold the balance and to keep the threefold flame of life for and on behalf of every living soul. It is the law of the One that the meditation of the one upon the Eternal Christos may count for the many until the many once again become accountable for their words and their works and can begin to bear the burden of their light as well as the karma of their relative good and evil.

"I chose to be that one. I volunteered to be a flaming son of righteousness unto earth and her evolutions."

That is how the picture of the so-called "rebellion of angels" is taking shape from different sources. The "rebellion" that took place in full conformity with the Cosmic Law. Everything in the material universe must be paid for. The salvation of humanity must be paid for as well. Someone had to sacrifice himself.

And, truly, it is quite cruel when humanity is besmirching the name of its Saviour during many centuries. The situation regarding this is more than unfair. Having received a chance to continue living, having obtained the Reason and the Fire of creation, humanity has been distorting its creative ability for centuries and blaming its Saviour for all its sins and disasters. And the first sin humanity blames its Saviour for is pridefulness. As a matter of fact, everyone is predisposed to see his own imperfections in another person. Only when watching the world through the prism of the distorted imperfect consciousness can man blame, for instance, Jesus for He, in His wish to rise to fame, allowed Himself to be crucified.

But the Saviour humbly takes the crucifixion upon Himself and has been bearing this burden during millions of years. And if, as Shakespeare said, "the time is out of joint", this joint must be regained. Sooner or later the truth will prevail.

"But, with the arts, the fire received has turned into the greatest curse: the animal element, and consciousness of its possession, has changed periodical instinct into chronic animalism and sensuality.[212] It is this which hangs over humanity like a heavy funereal pall. Thus arises the responsibility of free-will; the Titanic passions which represent humanity in its darkest aspect; 'the restless insatiability of the lower passions and desires, when, with self-asserting insolence, they bid defiance to the restraints of law'.[213]

"Prometheus having endowed man, according to Plato's 'Protagoras,' with that 'wisdom which ministers to physical wellbeing,' but the lower aspect of manas of the animal (Kama) having remained unchanged, instead of 'an untainted mind, heaven's first gift', there was created the eternal vulture of the ever unsatisfied desire, of regret and despair coupled with 'the dreamlike feebleness that fetters the blind race of mortals', unto the day when Prometheus is

---

[212] The animal world, having simple instinct to guide it, has its *seasons of procreation,* and the sexes become neutralized during the rest of the year. Therefore, the free animal knows sickness but once in its life – before it dies. (The footnote is copied from the book *The Secret Doctrine*)

[213] Introduction to "*Prometheus Bound,*" p. 152. (The footnote is copied from the book *The Secret Doctrine*)

released by his heaven-appointed deliverer, Herakles."[214]

"This, say Brahminical and Buddhistic legends, echoed by the Zoroastrian and now by the Christian teachings (the latter only occasionally), will happen at the end of Kaliyuga. It is only after the appearance of Kalki-Avatar, or Sosiosh, that man will be born from woman without sin. Then will Brahma, the Hindu deity; Ahura-Mazda (Ormazd), the Zoroastrian; Zeus, the Greco-Olympian Don Juan; Jehovah, the jealous, repenting, cruel, tribal God of the Israelites, and all their likes in the universal Pantheon of human fancy – vanish and disappear in thin air. And along with these will vanish their shadows, the dark aspects of all those deities, ever represented as their 'twin brothers' and creatures, in exoteric legend, their own reflection on earth – in esoteric philosophy. The Ahrimans and Typhons, the Samaels and Satans, must be all dethroned on that day, when every dark evil passion will be subdued.

"There is one eternal Law in nature, one that always tends to adjust contraries and to produce final harmony. It is owing to this law of spiritual development superseding the physical and purely intellectual, that mankind will become freed from its false gods, and find itself finally – SELF-REDEEMED.

"In its final revelation, the old myth of Prometheus – his proto- and anti-types being found in every ancient theogony – stands in each of them at the very origin of physical evil, because at the threshold of human physical life. KRONOS is 'Time,' whose first law is that the order of the successive and harmonious phases in the process of evolution during cyclic

---

[214] The Secret Doctrine, Vol. 2, p. 412-413

development should be strictly preserved – under the severe penalty of abnormal growth with all its ensuing results. It was not in the programme of natural development that man – higher animal though he may be – should become at once – intellectually, spiritually, and psychically – the demi-god he is on earth, while his physical frame remains weaker and more helpless and ephemeral than that of almost any huge mammal. The contrast is too grotesque and violent; the tabernacle much too unworthy of its indwelling god. The gift of Prometheus thus became a CURSE – though foreknown and foreseen by the HOST personified in that personage, as his name well shows[215]. It is in this that rests, at one and the same time, its sin and its redemption. For the Host that incarnated in a portion of humanity, though led to it by Karma or Nemesis, preferred free-will to passive slavery, intellectual self-conscious pain and even torture 'while myriad time shall flow' – to inane, imbecile, instinctual beatitude. Knowing such an incarnation was premature and not in the programme of nature, the heavenly host, 'Prometheus,' still sacrificed itself to benefit thereby, at least, one portion of mankind.[216] But while saving man from mental

---

[215] "As his name *Pro-me-theus*, meaning 'he who sees before him' or futurity, shows." (The Secret Doctrine, Vol. 2, p. 413.)

[216] Mankind is obviously divided into god-informed men and lower human creatures. The intellectual difference between the Aryan and other civilized nations and such savages as the South Sea Islanders, is inexplicable on any other grounds. No amount of culture, nor generations of training amid civilization, could raise such human specimens as the Bushmen, the Veddhas of Ceylon, and some African tribes, to the same intellectual level as the Aryans, the Semites, and the Turanians so called. The "sacred spark" is missing in them and it is they who are the only *inferior* races on the globe, now happily – owing to the wise adjustment of nature which ever works in that direction – fast dying out. Verily mankind is "of one blood," *but not of the same essence.* We are the hot-house,

darkness, they inflicted upon him the tortures of the self-consciousness of his responsibility – the result of his free will – besides every ill to which mortal man and flesh are heir to. This torture Prometheus accepted for himself, since the Host became henceforward blended with the tabernacle prepared for them, which was still unachieved at that period of formation.

"Spiritual evolution being incapable of keeping pace with the physical, once its homogeneity was broken by the admixture, the gift thus became the chief cause, if not the sole origin of Evil...[217]

"...In the case of Prometheus, Zeus represents the Host of the primeval progenitors, of the PITAR, the 'Fathers' who created man senseless and without any mind; while the divine Titan stands for the Spiritual creators, the devas who 'fell' into generation. The former are spiritually lower, but physically stronger, than the 'Prometheans': therefore, the latter are shown conquered. 'The lower Host, whose work the Titan spoiled and thus defeated the plans of Zeus,' was on this earth in its own sphere and plane of action; whereas, the superior Host was an exile from Heaven, who had got entangled in the meshes of matter. They (the inferior 'Host') were masters of all the Cosmic and lower titanic forces; the higher Titan possessed only the intellectual and spiritual fire. This drama of the struggle of Prometheus with the Olympic tyrant and despot, sensual Zeus, one sees enacted daily within our actual mankind: the lower passions chain the higher aspirations to the rock of matter, to

---

artificially quickened plants in nature, having in us a spark, which in them is latent. (The footnote is copied from the book *The Secret Doctrine*)

[217] The philosophical view of Indian metaphysics places the Root of Evil in the differentiation of the Homogeneous into the Heterogeneous, of the unit into plurality.

generate in many a case the vulture of sorrow, pain, and repentance."[218]

"*Man will rebecome the free Titan of old, but not before cyclic evolution has re-established the broken harmony between the two natures – the terrestrial and the divine; after which he becomes impermeable to the lower titanic forces, invulnerable in his personality, and immortal in his individuality, which cannot happen before every animal element is eliminated from his nature. When man understands that 'Deus non fecit mortem*'[219], *but that man has created it himself, he will re-become the Prometheus before his Fall.*"[220]

"*Volumes might be written, however, to no purpose for those who will neither see nor hear, except through the eyes and ears of their respective authorities.*"[221]

Conclusion

This publication had only one aim – to proclaim the Truth.

THE TRUTH MUST BE DIVULGED.

The good name of the Lightbearer, Lucifer, must be rehabilitated.

---

[218] The Secret Doctrine, Vol. 2, p. 420-422
[219] God did not create evil.
[220] The Secret Doctrine, Vol. 2, p. 422
[221] *Ibid.*, p. 409

Other books by Tatyana N. Mickushina

The books below contain the messages received by Tatyana N. Mickushina from the Ascended Masters.

Up to now there have been 20 books written and published in the Russian language.

The messages are constantly being translated into different languages by people all around the world. At present there are 19 languages that the messages are being translated into. The messages are also available online on the author's websites: **www.sirius-ru.net** (in Russian) and **www.sirius-eng.net** (in English).

In these books you will find the messages of the Masters of Wisdom, or the Ascended Masters, or the Masters of Shambala, or the Great White Brotherhood, or the Teachers of humanity, or the Hierarchy of the Forces of Light. They are known by different names. These beings have reached the next evolutionary step in their development.

The information contained in the messages belongs neither to any particular system of beliefs nor to any concrete religion.

The substance of these messages is that humanity is going through a very important stage of its development when it should give up focusing on the self, on the ego. It is necessary to transit to the new level of consciousness where man understands that he is not a mere physical body. At that level of consciousness man realises his Divine timeless nature, feels his interconnection with every living creature, with the entire universe. There arises a feeling of infinite Love, Compassion and Mercy towards everything that exists in space. At that level of consciousness such negative phenomena as hatred, wars, jealousy, vengeance, violence, ignorance, and fear are impossible.

And if in the near future humanity does not straighten its course in accordance with the stream of evolution, the most drastic consequences of its wrong collective choice are possible, even to the extent of a global cataclysm.

The messages of the Masters of Wisdom contain concrete recommendations on how humans should act in order to change their consciousness.

These messages are a helping hand extended through the worlds.

Words of Wisdom

This book was the first one. It contains all the Ascended Masters' messages received by Tatyana N. Mickushina in March – June, 2005.

Full-colour cover, paperback, 544 pages.

Words of Wisdom – 10

This book contains the messages given by the Ascended Masters during the summer cycle from June 20 to July 10, 2009. It also includes the messages of April 22 and May 24, 2009 and the messages published previously that are related to the content of the messages published in this book.

Full-colour cover, paperback, 110 pages.

The Masters about Karma

This book contains selected messages which were given by the Ascended Masters through their messenger Tatyana Mickushina from March 4, 2005 to January 10, 2007. In this book the Masters speak about karma. The knowledge about karma given by the Masters discloses the concept of karma from a new point of view.

Full-colour cover, paperback, 174 pages.

Good and Evil

An individual interpretation of *The Secret Doctrine*
by Helena P. Blavatsky

Tatyana N. Mickushina

Translated from Russian by
Svetlana Nekrasova

Proofreader: Alison Lobel

Author's websites:
http://sirius-eng.net (English version)
http://sirius-ru.net (Russian version)

For notes

Made in the USA
Charleston, SC
18 October 2010